ADVANCES IN
LIBRARY ADMINISTRATION
AND ORGANIZATION

Volume 4 • 1985

ADVANCES IN LIBRARY ADMINISTRATION AND ORGANIZATION

A Research Annual

Editors: **GERARD B. McCABE**
Director of Libraries
Clarion University of Pennsylvania

BERNARD KREISSMAN
University Librarian Emeritus
University of California, Davis

VOLUME 4 • 1985

 JAI PRESS INC.

Greenwich, Connecticut   *London, England*

CONTENTS

v

INTRODUCTION

Volume 4 of *Advances in Library Administration and Organization* continues the eclectic approach of the previous three volumes. The current volume addresses a multiplicity of administrative concerns ranging from statistics and management style to service to the disabled. The editors of ALAO intend to maintain the annual as a publication vehicle, as we noted in Volume 2, for meritorious "articles and research papers which either by their length or their nature would find other publication sources unreceptive."

Though this editorial policy would naturally tend to preclude a thematic volume devoted to a single major topic, strong managerial concerns do, nonetheless, run in trends, and one such tendency may indeed be noted in the current volume—the impact of technology on library operations. Technology in the management of libraries is very obviously a matter of current and growing interest for library managers, and that particular preoccupation is addressed in several of the following essays. One can predict that the particular concern of the application of technology to library operations, and its consequent impact on library management and administration, will not only continue but will grow in volume and depth. Looking forward, the next 10 years promise a revolution in information management practices that will have an impact on society greater than any previous development, with the possible exception of the invention of printing from movable type. It will be a magnificent decade for librarianship.

Looking backward to the late W. Carl Jackson's introduction

to Volume 1 of ALAO, it is interesting to note that the issues our predecessor raised as probable administrative concerns—collective bargaining, diminishing financial resources, automated operations and networking, professional responsibilities, alternatives to library construction, strengthened collection development policies, and preservation of our collections—have almost all been addressed in previous issues of ALAO, and several reappear in Volume 4. Thus we have evidence that regardless of the fact that each period brings one or two new overriding concerns, library managers must still deal with an extraordinary array of library issues. The editors of ALAO rededicate this annual publication to broad-ranging viewpoints and to all issues of concern to library administrators.

On a personal note, our dear friend and respected colleague Nelson A. Piper died on July 5, 1984. We dedicate these introductory pages to his memory.

Nelson A. Piper

October 5, 1925–July 5, 1984

Bernard Kreissman
Editor

THE THIRD CULTURE:
MANAGERIAL SOCIALIZATION IN THE LIBRARY SETTING

Ruth J. Person

INTRODUCTION

As library operations grow increasingly more complex, greater managerial involvement on the part of library personnel is very often required. Management in the library setting continues to evolve to cope with problems related to "coordination, adaptation, and organizational growth."[1] The overriding concern of management is with a so-called "action phase" of organizational life—with moving the organization from one place to another, figuratively speaking,[2] in order to maximize the organization's mission.

In *An Introduction to Management,* Litterer notes that "in order to understand managers, we need to know three kinds of

Advances in Library Administration and Organization, Volume 4, pages 1–24.
Copyright © 1985 by JAI Press Inc.
All rights of reproduction in any form reserved.
ISBN: 0-89232-566-6

things: (1) what they manage (i.e., organizations); (2) the knowledge and skills they use to manage them (i.e., technology); and (3) "how they look at the world and themselves and think about problems (i.e., culture)."[3]

In identifying and defining the term *culture* as it relates to management, Litterer also suggests that management is a *third* culture, apart from science and the humanities. Expanding on C. P. Snow's "Two Cultures," Litterer suggests that management involves processes that run counter to the first two cultures (Such as making compromises and tolerating uncertainty and imprecision) and that in fact it assumes its own world view, rules, technology, and identifiable membership.[4]

Library management literature addresses the nature of library organizations and the technology of library management. Little discussion, however, has been directed at the third area—the nature of managerial culture—and the process of socialization that accompanies it. It can be observed that, in the library setting, acculturation is not particularly easy, since it takes place within a professional organization context in which there are bound to be conflicting professional and managerial views, values, and norms.

However, over a period of time, librarians who assume managerial responsibility learn what is expected of a library manager, what the managerial role entails, and what is appropriate to the Third Culture. According to Schein, this "managerial socialization" process is primarily one of "learning the ropes." In this process, the individual is "indoctrinated and trained . . . and taught what is important"[5] in terms of managerial behavior. While organizational socialization has been defined as "those changes caused by the organization that take place in newcomers,"[6] managerial socialization may be even more subtle, relating specifically to the way the managerial (rather than merely the organizational) culture changes newcomers to the managerial role. Wanous suggests that the socialization process itself within organizations consists of several phases, including (1) confronting reality, (2) achieving role clarity, and (3) detecting signposts of successful socialization.[7]

Using these phases as a possible model, it could be observed that some library managers move through the socialization process successfully, developing great interest in and commitment to management and adopting wholeheartedly the managerial role. There are others, however, who may reject the managerial role. A third group may be unsure of their stance and be unable to achieve role clarity and successful socialization.

The importance of the managerial socialization process cannot be underestimated. According to Schein, "the process is so ubiquitous and we go through it so often during our total career, that it is all too easy to overlook it. Yet it is a process which can make or break a career, and which can make or break organizational systems of manpower planning."[8] Because librarianship lacks a formal means of socializing managers, each individual "learns the ropes" as best as he/she can. There is no widely-accepted program of study for individuals who must assume managerial responsibility in libraries, nor are there clearly defined paths within library organizations that provide a structured means of socialization. Compounding this problem is the lack of a widely-accepted body of knowledge about what a library manager *does*. Thus, most librarians who assume a managerial role receive little structured preparation or guidance for that role.

STUDYING MANAGERIAL SOCIALIZATION IN LIBRARIES

To explore the managerial socialization process among library managers, a study was designed to examine sources of managerial role definition used by individuals who hold managerial responsibility in libraries below the level of director or assistant director and to identify the major phases in their socialization process.

Subjects were drawn from 15 large academic and public libraries located in a particular geographic region. These libraries represented institutions with more than 50 professional staff members and were relatively complex organizations in which the nature of the organization's work and the resulting size of the organization necessitated an organizational structure with multiple managerial levels. Such organizations included both ARL academic libraries and major city and city/county public libraries. While the clients served by these libraries are admittedly different, the size and complexity of the organizations were quite similar.

After all eligible individuals were contacted about their possible participation, 75 percent (150 subjects) participated in the study. These individuals were largely department heads, branch heads, and staff coordinators who occupied positions identified as "middle management" by their libraries. They included individuals who were at various stages in the socialization process.

Data necessary to complete the research were of two types— objective and subjective. Using both types of data collection allowed the gathering of information of both a factual and an attitudinal nature, and provided an opportunity to cross-check information for accuracy of understanding and interpretation.

Objective data consisted of two types: (1) organizational information received through the distribution of a factual questionnaire to directors of the participating libraries, and (2) personal information received through the distribution of an extensive questionnaire to each participating subject.

Subjective data consisted of personal expressions of the subjects regarding their perceptions of their managerial role. This data was collected by means of personal interviews with each subject, since appropriate methods of ascertaining managers' perceptions of managerial socialization were not readily available in questionnaire format. Much of the information necessary to provide an accurate picture of these perceptions required interpretation in order to be properly elicited from subjects. Therefore, the face-to-face interview technique was used. Personal interviews were conducted with all 150 participating subjects by one interviewer at each subject's place of work.

RESULTS OF THE STUDY:
LEARNING TO BE A LIBRARY MANAGER

Sources of Role Definition

Through both the written questionnaire and the interview sources of role definition for library managers were identified. These were categorized into four groups and ranked in order of their importance to the subjects.

Personal Sources

Library managers come in contact with many individuals who are potential sources of information about managerial role behavior. These can include relatives, friends, coworkers at present and past organizations, professional colleagues, community leaders—in short, anyone who has served in a managerial capacity, who has a special interest in management, or who merely has an opinion about management (see Figure 1). Not only might some of these individuals serve as actual role models, both positive and negative, for the library manager, but others might influence his/her ideas about appropriate role behavior simply by communicating their own expectations, thoughts, or feelings.

These potential role senders were identified in two categories: (present) work-related contacts, and nonwork contacts. Subjects were asked first about work-related contacts which they made in carrying out their managerial responsibilities, and then about additional individuals with whom they discussed managerial work or management in general outside of working relationships. In attempting to categorize role senders in this way, it is of course virtually impossible to establish a mutually exclusive set of criteria. Thus, a working colleague may also be a personal friend, so it would sometimes be difficult to separate work-related from purely personal discussion.

Almost all of the subjects indicated that carrying out their managerial responsibilities required regular contact with other individuals who might serve as role senders. These potential role senders included: managerial peers, superiors, subordinates, members of other library service groups with whom coordination was required, members of the parent organization (such as personnel officers, deans of academic units, and the like) and other outsiders in the larger work-related community such as citizen group members, members of cooperative organizations to which the library belonged, and others with whom work relationships were necessary.

All library managers in the survey reported formally to some other individual or individuals within the library. In most cases, this was the library director or assistant director. Twenty-seven individuals reported formally to two superiors. One-quarter of the managers had working contact with *all* categories of potential role senders in the work place, as indicated in Table 1. In moving farther away from the library itself, however, the inclusion of library-external role senders as working contacts decreased. While 67 percent of the managers had contact with peers in the library, only 45 percent worked directly with other library service

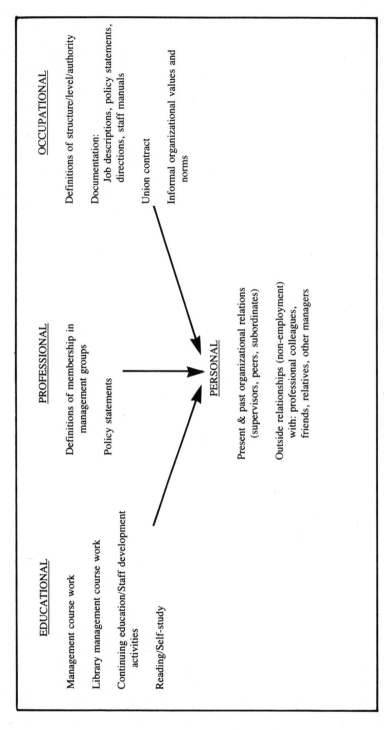

Figure 1. Examples of Potential Sources of Managerial Role Definition and Concepts.

Table 1. Work-Related Contacts with Potential Role Senders

Type of Role Sender	Percentage Including Contact
All types	26
Peers (library)	67
Other service groups (library)	45
Parent organization members	35
Work-related outsiders	22

units, and a considerably fewer number came in contact with "outsiders" on a regular basis.

In spite of the fact that the potential for making community or "outside" contacts in the public library might seem greater, academic library managers reported just as many "outside" potential role senders in the work environment as did their public library counterparts. A number of public library managers indicated a dissatisfaction with their inability to establish and maintain these kinds of relationships in the larger workplace due to organizational climate in the library and top-management constraints.

At the more personal (nonwork) level, three-quarters of the subjects indicated that there were additional individuals who either were or had been important to them personally with whom they discussed managerial work. The majority of these role senders were individuals with whom the manager came in contact as a result of personal friendship, family relationships, or professional and community involvement.

By far, most of these nonwork members of the managers' role sets were personal friends or family members. It was clear from interview data that while the female managers included members of both sexes in their nonwork role set, male managers almost exclusively confined their role set to other males. A number of women referred to themselves as "classic cases" of female managers (first-born daughters of fathers who had held managerial positions). Some of these women as well as others in the survey had spouses who held managerial positions with whom they discussed the practice of management.

Male library managers, on the other hand, rarely named spouses or female parents as potential role senders, but more often named other family members such as brothers or male cousins who held managerial positions. They also named close male friends as important members of their nonwork role set. Some male subjects had been able to form relationships with other individuals in the community who became important members of their role set through involvement in organizations such as the Jaycees.

In summary, interview data clearly suggested that the majority of the managers in the study included not only a sizeable number of work-related contacts in their role set, but also outside individuals who provided them with a means of exploring appropriate managerial role behavior and expectations. In 1970, some 50 percent of the library administrators surveyed by Wasserman and Bundy[9] indicated that they were influenced by a librarian they knew in choosing librarianship as a career. In studying the networks that managers form in carrying out managerial responsibilities, Kaplan and Mazique also note the sizeable number of personal contacts made by managers and the diversity of these person-to-person transactions.[10] The present study data indicated again that individual influence is very important. Thus, in helping the library manager formulate concepts and develop perceptions of managerial role definition and behavior, personal sources ranked first of the four major areas explored.

Occupational Sources and Managerial Experience

Through documentation such as job descriptions, staff manuals, and policy statements, as well as by organizational structure itself (along with structural definitions of membership and characteristics of various levels), the individual's present or past employing organization may provide important sources of role formalization and definition. In the unionized setting, additional documentation such as the union contract may serve to increase the formalization and definition of the managerial role.

In spite of the potential of such documentation, less than one-third of the subjects indicated that such information was available, or if available, was helpful in providing definitions of the managerial role. Those who did report such helpfulness indicated that job descriptions and staff manuals were the most useful sources of definition to them. These sources provided information primarily about the kinds of activities in which managers in their organization should be involved.

Two other potential sources—definitions related to organizational structure, and union contracts—proved relatively unimportant to the subjects. Only half of the libraries surveyed had formal, written definitions of management levels and only one third of the libraries had unions, most of which were for maintenance and support workers.

Previous management experience can also contribute to the development of managerial role concepts (Table 2). Subjects reported a mean of 7.5 years of positional tenure, and approximately five years of previous managerial experience. This reported previous management experience could be further subdivided: slightly less than half of the subjects had had one previous managerial position, while one-fourth had held more than one such previous position. While a high precentage of the subjects were well prepared for their present position in terms of previous experience, nearly one-third had had *no* previous managerial experience of any kind, moving directly from professional work into managerial responsibility at the middle level.

Further analysis of previous management positions of the subjects revealed that movement *between* libraries at the managerial level was limited. Of the subjects with experience, sixty percent had gained such experience at the same library in which they were employed at the time of the study. While this indicated some movement between libraries, there appeared to be only a small amount of cross-fertilization between the two *types* of li-

Table 2. Previous Management Experience

Positional tenure (years)	7.5
Previous management experience (years)	5.0
Previous number of managerial positions:	
None	30%
One	45%
Multiple	25%
Location of previous managerial positions:	
Same library	60%
Different library or Non-library organization	40%

braries included in the study, since even the individuals who had had experience outside their own library tended to have worked in a similar type of library.

Educational Sources

In the professions, education is a major source of role definition and socialization. Through the first professional degree in library science, entrants to librarianship learn not only about the nature of the profession, but also hopefully develop some sense of "professional community."

In this context, subjects were asked a number of questions related to their educational attainments in order to ascertain whether any information about the nature of managerial work and role behavior might have been derived from educational endeavors. Since educational preparation is one of the primary entrance requirements to librarianship, it was expected that educational activities would rank first as sources of role definition for library managers in the study.

Educating oneself for the assumption of a managerial role in the library setting can take a variety of directions. These directions can be represented by a continuum of managerial education based on formality, as identified in Figure 2. In the most formal or structured sense, individuals may seek degrees in non-library-related management programs, most common of which would be the M.B.A., M.P.A., or M.S. in Administration. A less structured approach would be enrollment in general management or library management course work either during a first professional degree program or at some later date. In the more informal sense, there are a number of opportunities for librarians interested in developing managerial knowledge, skills, and competencies. Such opportunities exist through staff development programs within the individual's workplace or through outside agencies such as associations, library schools, business schools, and private firms. On a more self-directed level, activities such as reading management-related literature may also provide information about managerial role behavior.

In spite of initial expectations, the first professional degree experience did not serve to any great extent as a means of socialization about the nature of the *managerial* aspects of library

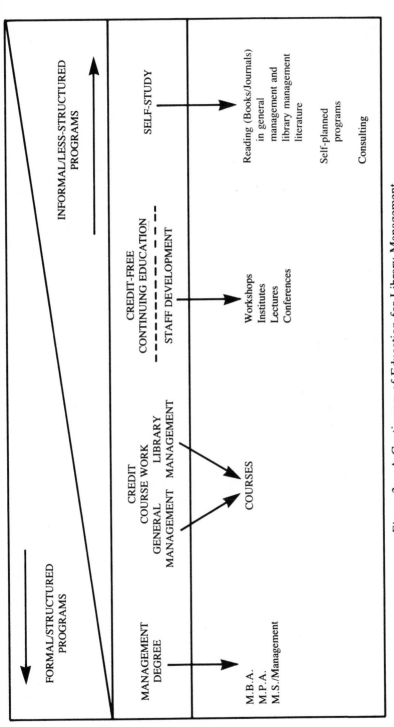

Figure 2. A Continuum of Education for Library Management.

Table 3. Degree-Related Educational Attainments

Degree	Percentage Having Degree
No degree	1
Bachelor's degree only	2
Fifth-Year B.L.S. only	8
M.L.S.	83
Subject Master's	22
Other Master's (professional)	3
Doctorate	6

work for this particular group of librarians who had moved through various levels of professional work to a managerial level. While more than 80 percent of the subjects held the M.L.S. degree or its equivalent, (see Table 3) only 10 percent of these subjects developed an interest in library management while attending library school. Only half of the individuals in the sample had ever taken a library administration course. Of these, only 35 percent indicated that the course was helpful in developing their knowledge of managerial role behavior and responsibilities.

While individuals might forget the exact nature and content of course work taken in the past, most subjects in the study were in fact able to indicate their reasons for negative assessment of library administration courses taken. Answers were given in three categories: (1) the focus was on practical ("how-to-do-it") aspects of management, with little attempt to link these aspects to managerial role behavior, (2) instructors focused largely on their experiences in a particular library, with the result that students learned a great deal about one or two library operations but little about general managerial role behavior, and (3) course emphasis was on management as a process, neglecting the individual manager's role in that process and the kinds of role behavior that are appropriate for different managerial levels in libraries. Thus a potentially helpful and important source of role definition, certainly one which is available to almost all potential library managers was either not utilized or not found to be helpful by over 80 percent of the library managers surveyed.

Few managers chose the most formal approach to learning about management—the management degree (Table 4). Only two individuals held the M.B.A. degree, and one an undergraduate

Table 4.   Management-Related Educational Involvements

Activity	Participation (% participating in activity)	
	No Activity	One + Activity
Library administration course(s) (credit)	50	50
Management course(s) (credit)	85	15
Continuing education/ staff development	52 65	48 35
Self-study: Reading management/ library management books Reading management journals Reading management articles in library journals	67 92 24	33 8 76

degree in business. In addition, five others had taken three or more management courses outside the field of library science. The option of course work taken at the discretion of the individual (rather than as part of a formal degree program) was utilized in two ways: first, by individuals who enrolled in non-library-related management courses, and second by individuals who had enrolled in library management courses. A number of subjects commented on the scarcity of *library*-related management courses available through library schools beyond the introductory level.

The most positive responses about helpfulness of education came from the individuals who had enrolled in non-library-management course work. Of the 22 individuals who had taken such courses, 19 indicated that they provided an opportunity to learn about managerial role behavior and managerial responsibility. While these courses approached management from the business setting, subjects indicated that for the most part they were able to make the translation to the library setting without difficulty. Negative comments from three subjects indicated that they expected such translation to be made *for* them.

In gathering information about participation in the less formal or less-structured approaches to managerial education, a two-part approach was used. First, subjects were asked to identify the kinds of credit-free continuing education activities related to management (such as seminars, workshops, institutes and the like) in which they had been involved during the five years preceding the study *at their own initiative*. About half of the subjects had been involved in some activity of this kind. For the most part, these activities dealt with the "human skills" areas of management (such as communication, motivation, supervisory skills) as opposed to those of a more technical (such as accounting) or conceptual (such as planning) nature. While the majority of these programs were sponsored by a library organization or institution, a number of individuals indicated that through outside involvements (such as Jaycees, reserve military duty, religious groups, and the like) they had been able to participate in managerial training activities which had applicability in many kinds of managerial situations.

Library managers were also asked about their participation in staff development programs (those sponsored by the individual's library or the library's parent organization). During the five years prior to the study, only about one-third of the subjects had participated in a management-related activity of this kind. For the most part, the individuals who had participated in such activity represented two libraries, each of which had sponsored a program for management staff in cooperation with the parent organization. Again, these activities were largely related to the "human skills" areas of management.

The final category under educational sources is that of "self-study"—the kinds of independent, informal review of literature and the like that one would do on one's own. While few individuals used management journals as a source of study, about one-third did utilize management and library management books in this way and more than three-fourths used articles in library periodicals as a source of managerial information.

Subjects who utilized formal business or public administration courses judged them most helpful when they enrolled close to the time at which such information might be used in a job situation. This relationship suggests that the "need to know" approach may have particular merit in viewing the role of education in the socialization process of library management personnel. Following this theme, greater numbers of library managers might be expected to enroll in continuing education and staff development programs which would be more useful at a practical level. However, in reality, only about half of the subjects had participated in continuing education activity related to management; only about one-third had participated in any similar staff development activity. In addition, of those who *had* participated, many indicated that they were not particularly helpful. "Self-study" appeared to be a much more utilized and helpful form of education for most of the subjects.

Professional Sources

Professional, managerial, and service membership associations can serve also as a potential source of role definition for library managers. Position and policy statements, definitions of membership in managerial subgroups, development of professional contacts and provision of educational programs are all means of identifying appropriate managerial role behavior. Responses from this study, however, indicated that this potential source of role definition fared poorly, ranking fourth. Membership itself was low in both management associations and groups within library associations. Only two subjects belonged to management associations; a few male subjects belonged to service organizations such as the Jaycees. Few subjects even belonged to management groups within library associations.

Even in an indirect sense, associations fared poorly—few subjects rated association-sponsored educational programs helpful in role definition, and few indicated that personal sources of role definition included contacts made *specifically* through library associations.

Patterns of Role Adoption

In reviewing the data collected on a case-by-case basis, rather than in the aggregate, patterns of role adoption emerged. Three criteria were specifically used to determine level of role adoption: (1) level of interest expressed in management compared to the non-managerial aspects of library work, (2) reason for taking present position being the desire for more managerial responsibility, and (3) level of involvement in managerial versus non-managerial activity on the job.

Using these criteria, twenty-six individuals emerged as what might be called "high-interest" managers and twenty-seven as "low-interest" managers. The remainder of the subjects were categorized as "split-interest" managers who divided their identification between managerial and nonmanagerial roles. Because the high interest managers represented examples of *successful socialization,* the study concentrated on identifying characteristics related to their role adoption.

Sixteen of these high-interest individuals were women, while 10 were men; 10 represented public libraries, and 16 the academic setting. Looking more closely at the individual characteristics of this group, it was apparent that they differed from their managerial peers in several important ways.

First, these managers indicated that they attributed their interest and participation in management to a combination of "working with people" *and* "solving complex problems in an organizational setting" (which to many of them included people-related problems). McCall has confirmed both the people-related and problem-solving dimensions as important differences between managerial and professional work;[11] these high-interest managers were able to readily discern such differences, while their split-interest and low-interest counterparts were not.

Second, while there was no *one* discernable educational path which these managers followed in reaching their present position, some common directions existed. All held the first professional degree in library science; the majority had taken a course at some time in library management as well. All had been involved in one or more continuing education activity in the five years preceding the study; all also used "self-study" quite extensively as a means of learning more about library management. In spite of this level of involvement, most of these managers indicated a desire for even greater levels of activity in managerial education in the future.

Third, the "high-interest" manager's role set was *highly* diverse—consisting of contacts in *all* four work-related categories as well as an unusually high number of non-work related contacts who might influence managerial perceptions and concepts. Such contacts included a wide array of spouses, parents, relatives, and long-time personal friends who held managerial positions. Many of these contacts were from the business sector, education, or human services. These managers indicated that they derived great benefit from "talking over" both general work-related managerial concerns and ideas about how the managerial role should be approached with these personal contacts.

Fourth, because of their low involvement in non-managerial activity, role dimension for these managers tended to be somewhat narrower in the overall sense than that of their peers. In other words, their managerial role was restricted largely to management-related areas of concern rather than encompassing more of the nonmanagerial aspects of library work such as reference or cataloging work. In addition, these managers were often able to delegate some of their internally-directed managerial activities to other unit members, leaving them freer to concentrate on involvement in the more external aspects of the managerial role.

While causal relationship cannot necessarily be inferred in this examination of "high interest" managers, it is nevertheless important to recognize the emergence of a group of library managers with characteristics that indicate an overriding concern with the practice of management in the library setting. The fact that these individuals possessed a common set of general characteristics with respect to role set, role dimension, and educational endeavor suggested that other librarians who wish to achieve successful socialization might do well to cultivate these characteristics.

The Managerial Socialization Process

In reviewing recent work on stage models of organizational socialization, Wanous combined several well-known approaches into an integrative model.[12] His first three stages of socialization ("confronting and accepting organizational reality," "achieving role clarity," and "locating oneself in the organizational context") refer to the socialization process itself. The fourth stage ("detecting signposts of successful socialization") indicates the transition of the individual from newcomer to insider.

Continuing the individual case-by-case analysis suggested in the previous section, both questionnaire and interview data were examined to ascertain whether in fact the managers in this study followed similar paths to those suggested by Wanous for the larger organizational socialization process. With some notable exceptions relating primarily to the nature of professional organizations and the particular difficulty individuals trained as professionals have in relinquishing technical expertise, the socialization process proved to be quite similar to that suggested by Wanous.

Since Wanous focused on *successful* socialization in his model, the analysis for the present study focused mainly on the "high interest" managers who represented the greatest degree of successful managerial socialization. The process outlined in Figure 3 was for them an evolutionary one which focused not so much on the passsage of time as on certain crucial and homogeneous events in their careers as managers.

In *Leadership and the Professional,* McCall clearly summed up the dilemma facing professionals in organizations who consider moving into management. The flow of power to administrators in professional bureaucracies, the belief that success lies in management, and the escape from professional obsolescence are all compelling reasons for choosing the managerial track.[13] Yet the differences between managerial and professional work are enormous, as studies on the use of time by both groups have demonstrated.[14]

The "high interest" managers in the present study were able to identify these potential differences in roles in a process similar to that of Lewin's "unfreezing"[15] after defining their clear interest in management. They were also able to utilize a wide variety of role definition sources to confirm/disconfirm expectations about managerial realities. Interview data also indicated that through struggle, hard work, educational endeavors, self-study, and above all self-examination, these managers were able to achieve role clarity and establish themselves in the organizational context as managers. The generally high levels of satisfaction with the managerial role, expressed organizational commitment, and indications of a balanced level of involvement in the managerial working roles (combined with a disinclination toward involvement in nonmanagerial work) suggested that these "high-interest" managers had achieved successful socialization.

At the other end of the spectrum, "low-interest" managers expressed much less satisfaction with their work, particularly with the need to relinquish often-cherished non-managerial activities. Unlike their "high-interest" counterparts, who had taken their present positions largely because they represented an increase in responsibility and challenge, these managers had ac-

Figure 3:   Stages in the Managerial Socialization Process. *Identified by
Wanous.[16]

Stage 1: Confronting and Accepting Reality
  (a) Identifying a clear interest in management and seeking sources of role
      definition (especially personal and professional)
  (b) Unfreezing of technical commitment to a particular aspect of the
      profession (i.e. reference work, cataloging, etc.)
 *(c) Confirming/disconfirming expectations
  (d) Understanding professional/bureaucratic conflicts and *possible per-
      sonal/organizational conflicts

Stage 2: Achieving Role Clarity (Internalization)
 *(a) Being initiated to tasks in managerial job
 *(b) Defining interpersonal roles with boss, present peers, former peers
      and professional colleagues in the organization, and subordinates
  (c) Identifying and establishing patterns of involvement in the 10 man-
      agerial working roles
  (d) Seeking additional sources of role definition (especially educational
      and occupational)
 *(e) Congruence between personal and organizational evaluation of man-
      agerial performance
 *(f) Learning how to work with both structure and ambiguity

Stage 3: Locating Oneself in the Organizational Context
 *(a) Learning which modes of one's behavior are congruent with those
      expected of managers in the organization
  (b) *resolution of conflicts at work, and between outside professional
      interests and managerial demands
  (c) Establishment of an altered self-image, new interpersonal relation-
      ships, and adoption of new values

Stage 4: Detecting Signposts of Successful Socialization
 *(a) Organizational commitment
 *(b) High satisfaction
 *(c) Job involvement

cepted managerial jobs primarily because they represented a salary increase and a chance for promotion. In other words, money
and upward movement in the organization were most important
to these managers, rather than an interest in management itself.
These managers expressed generally low levels of satisfaction
with their jobs, and in some cases found the management re-

sponsibilities assigned to them to be merely a hindrance to their more preferred work—reference, cataloging, acquisitions, and the like.

CONCLUSION

It was readily apparent that managers in the study made the greatest use of their own interpersonal and individual means of managerial socialization, particularly through personal sources and self-study, as opposed to more structured or group approaches gained through educational programs, professional, or organizational influences or documentation. A cautionary note is important, however. While personal contacts can be a rich source of role definition, these individuals may often come from the manager's own library setting or from similar organizations. Thus the possibility exists that a rather insular view of library management may develop if personal sources of definition are largely confined to the same type of library setting or to the organization itself.

Neither libraries nor library education made the development of role concepts by the library managers in this study particularly easy. No clear path of study was provided by library education for potential and actual incumbents in the management role to follow in developing either management knowledge and skills or appropriate notions about role behavior. Libraries were somewhat lax in formalizing roles through organizational documentation as basic as definitions of levels or useful job descriptions. They were also remiss in providing opportunities for staff development of management personnel so that role behavior might have been examined more thoroughly. Library associations, which have a dual responsibility not only to provide a source of managerial education through programming and publication as well as to encourage individual library organizations to formalize roles and provide helpful organizational documentation for employees, did not undertake this responsibility in a way which was helpful to the managerial personnel in the present study. It was left largely to the individual library managers surveyed to seek information about managerial role behavior, largely from personal sources and self-study efforts.

It is incumbent upon library education and library associations to provide means of cross-fertilization of ideas outside the organizational context; it is also important that library organizations themselves increase the opportunities for developing personal sources of role definition outside the confines of the library itself if views of library management are to be broadened and enriched. At the same time, libraries have a responsibility to provide adequate means of role formalization so that role clarity can be achieved by the majority of managers in any given organization. Individuals themselves also have a responsibility to avail themselves of opportunities for development and to clarify for themselves the choices they must make between professional and managerial work.

NOTES

1. Joseph A. Litterer, *An Introduction to Management* (New York: Wiley, 1978), p. 9.
2. Litterer, p. 10.
3. Litterer, p. 3.
4. Litterer, pp. 10–11.
5. Edgar H. Schein, "Organizational Socialization and the Profession of Management." *Industrial Management Review* (Winter 1968, p. 2.)
6. John P. Wanous, *Organizational Entry: Recruitment, Selection, and Socialization of Newcomers* (Reading, Mass.: Addison-Wesley, 1980), p. 168.
7. Wanous, p. 180.
8. Schein, p. 2.
9. Mary Lee Bundy and Paul Wasserman, *The Academic Library Administrator and His Situation* (Washington, D.C.: U.S. Department of Health, Education, and Welfare [now U.S. Department of Education], 1970), p. 13.
10. Robert E. Kaplan and Mignon Mazique, *Trade Routes: The Manager's Network of Relationships* (Greensboro, N.C.: Center for Creative Leadership, 1983), p. 2.
11. Morgan W. McCall, Jr., *Leadership and the Professional* (Greensboro, N.C.: Center for Creative Leadership, 1981), p. 22.
12. Wanous, p. 180.
13. McCall, p. 22.
14. McCall, p. 22.
15. Kurt Lewin, "Frontiers in Group Dynamics: Concept, Method, and Reality in Social Science; Social Equilibria and Social Change." *Human Relations* 1 (June 1947), pp. 5–41.
16. Wanous, p. 180.

REFERENCES

Bayton, James A. and Chapman, Richard L. "Making Managers of Scientists and Engineers." *The Bureaucrat* 1 (Winter 1972):407–425.

Bell, Robert R. and Keyes, J. Bernard. "Preparing for a Move to Middle Management." *Supervisory Management* 25 (July 1980):10–16.

Berlew, D. W. and Hall, D. T. "The Socialization of Managers: Effects of Expectations on Performance." *Administrative Science Quarterly* 11 (September 1966):207-233.

Branch, Jan and Wiles, Marilyn. "Beyond Gatekeeping: An Anthropological View of What Follows Entry." *Educational Horizons* 55 (Spring 1977):140–145.

Bray, D. W., Campbell, R. J., and Grant, D. L. *Formative Years in Business.* New York: Wiley, 1974.

Broadwell, Martin. "Moving Up to Supervision." *Training & Development Journal* 33 (February 1979):12–18.

Buchanan, B. "Building Organizational Commitment: The Socialization of Managers in Work Organizations." *Administrative Science Quarterly* 19 (1974):533-546.

Couch, Peter D. "Learning to be a Middle Manager." *Business Horizons* 22 (February 1979):33–41.

———. Some Effects of Training and Experience on Concepts of Supervision. Ph.D. Dissertation, University of Wisconsin, 1965.

Crowe, Bruce R. "The Effects of Subordinate's Behavior on Managerial Style." *Human Relations* 25 (July 1972):215–237.

Feldman, Daniel Charles. "Contingency Theory of Socialization." *Administrative Science Quarterly* 21 (September 1976):433–452.

———. "The Multiple Socialization of Organization Members." *Academy of Management Review* 6 (April 1981):309–318.

———. "A Socialization Process That Helps New Recruits Succeed." *Personnel* (March-April 1980):11–23.

———. "The First Job: Making the Transition to Manager." S.A.M. *Advanced Management Journal* 43 (Autumn 1978):54–60.

Gabarro, John. "Socialization at the Top—How CEO's and Subordinates Evolve Interpersonal Contracts." *Organizational Dynamics* 7 (Winter 1979):3–23.

Graen, George. "Role Making Processes Within Complex Organizations." In *Handbook of Industrial and Organizational Psychology,* ed. by Marvin Dunnette. Chicago: Rand McNally, 1976 (pp. 1201–1245).

Greene, Charles N. "Identification Modes of Professionals: Relationship With Formalization, Role Strain, and Alienation." *Academy of Management Journal* 21 (1978):486–492.

Haga, W. J. "Managerial Professionalism and the Use of Organizational Resources." *American Journal of Economics and Sociology* 35 (October 1976):337–348.

Hall, Douglas T. *Careers in Organizations.* Pacific Palisades, CA: Goodyear, 1976.

———. "A Theoretical Model of Career Subidentity Development in Organizational Settings." *Organizational Behavior and Human Performance* 6 (1971):50–76.

Izareli, D. N. "The Middle Manager and the Tactics of Power—a Case Study." *Sloan Management Review* 16 (Winter 1975):59–70.

Kanter, Rosabeth Moss. "The Middle Manager as Innovator." *Harvard Business Review* (July-August 1982):95–105.

Kaplan, Robert E. and Mazique, Mignon. *Trade Routes: The Manager's Network of Relationships.* Greensboro, N.C.: Center for Creative Leadership, 1983.

Katz, R. "Job Longevity as a Situational Factor in Job Satisfaction." *Administrative Science Quarterly* 23 (June 1978):204–223.

Kipnis, Davis, Schmidt, Stuart M., and Wilkinson, Ian. "Intra-organizational Influence Tactics: Explorations in Getting One's Way." *Journal of Applied Psychology* 65 (August 1980):440–452.

Kok, J. and Strable, E. G. "Moving Up: A Study of Librarians Who Have Become Officers in Their Organizations." New York: Special Libraries Association, 1979 (Selected Papers of the 70th Annual Conference of the Special Libraries Association, 1979, Fiche 79–03).

Lebell, D. "Managing Professionals: The Quiet Conflict. *Personnel Journal* 59 (1980):566–572.

Lee, Susan A. "Conflict and Ambiguity in the Role of the Academic Library Director." *College & Research Libraries* 38 (September 1977):396–403.

Lewin, Kurt. "Frontiers in Group Dynamics: Concept, Method, and and Reality in Social Science; Social Equilibria and Social Change." *Human Relations* 1 (June 1947):5–41.

Light, D. "Surface Data and Deep Structure: Observing the Organization of Professional Training." *Administrative Science Quarterly* 24 (December 1979):551–559.

Litterer, Joseph A. *An Introduction to Management.* New York: Wiley, 1978.

McAnally, Arthur M. and Downs, Robert B. "The Changing Role of Directors of University Libraries." *College & Research Libraries* (March 1973):103–125.

McCall, Morgan W. Jr. *Leadership and the Professional.* Greensboro, N.C.: Center for Creative Leadership, 1981.

McCall, Morgan W. Jr. and Segrist, Cheryl A. *In Pursuit of the Manager's Job: Building on Mintzberg.* Greensboro, N.C.: Center for Creative Leadership, 1980.

Metz, Paul. "Administrative Succession in the Academic Library." *College & Research Libraries* 39 (September 1978):358–365.

———. "The Role of the Academic Library Director." *Journal of Academic Librarianship* 5 (July 1979):148–152.

Miller, G. A. and Wager, L. W. "Adult Socialization, Organizational Structure, and Role Orientations." *Administrative Science Quarterly* 16 (June 1971):151–163.

Moore, M. L. "Superior, Self, and Subordinate Differences in Perceptions of Managerial Learning Times." *Personnel Psychology* 27 (1974):297—305.

Murray, Thomas J. "More Power for the Middle Manager." *Dun's Review* 111 (June 1978):60–62.

Neff, Thomas J. "Bridging the Promotion Gap." *Management Review* 67 (January 1978):42–45.

Ondrach, D. A. "Socialization in Professional Schools: A Comparative Study." *Administrative Science Quarterly* 20 (March 1975):97–103; (December 1975):631–633.

Pearse, Robert F. *Manager to Manager: What Managers Think of Management Development.* New York: American Management Association, 1977.

———. *Manager to Manager II: What Managers Think of Their Managerial Careers.* New York: American Management Association, 1977.

Pfann, Robert L. "Neither Fish Nor Fowl." *Personnel Journal* 54 (March 1975):149, 176–177.

Pheysey, D. C. "Managers' Occupational Histories, Organizational Environments, and Climates for Management Development." *Journal of Management Studies* 14 (February 1977):58–79.

Plate, Kenneth H. and Seigel, J. P. "Career Patterns of Ontario Librarians." *Canadian Library Journal* 36 (June 1979):143–148.

Rothman, Robert A. and Perrucci, Robert. "Organizational Careers and Professional Expertise." *Administrative Science Quarterly* 15 (September 1970):282–293.

Schein, Edgar H. *Career Dynamics.* Reading, Mass.: Addison-Wesley, 1978.

———. "Organizational Socialization and the Profession of Management." *Industrial Management Review* (Winter 1968):1–16.

———. "Attitude Change During Management Education: A Study of Organizational Influences on Student Attitudes." *Administrative Science Quarterly* 11 (1967):601–628.

Slusher, Allen; VanDyke, James; and Rose, Gerald. "Technical Competence of Group Leaders, Managerial Roles, and Productivity in Engineering Design Groups." *Academy of Management Journal* (June 1972):197–204.

Stead, Bette Ann and Scammell, Richard W. "A Study of the Relationship of Role Conflict, the Need for Role Clarity, and Job Satisfaction for Professional Librarians." *Library Quarterly* 50 (July 1980):310–323.

Thompson, Harvey A. and Waters, James A. "Taking Over the New Job: Breaking Through Versus Breaking In." *S.A.M. Advanced Management Journal* 44 (Spring 1979):4–16.

Van Maanen, John. "People Processing: Strategies of Organizational Socialization." *Organizational Dynamics* (Summer 1978):13–36.

———. "Rookie Cops and Rookie Managers." *Wharton Magazine* 1 (1976):49–55.

Wanous, John P. *Organizational Entry: Recruitment, Selection, and Socialization of Newcomers.* Reading, Mass.: Addison-Wesley, 1980.

Weiss, Howard M. "Subordinate Imitation of Supervisor Behavior: The Role of Modeling in Organizational Socialization." *Organizational Behavior and Human Performance* 19 (1977):89–105.

Zierden, William E. "Needed: Top Management Attention to the Role of the First-Line Supervisor." *S.A.M. Advanced Management Journal* 45 (Summer 1980):18–25.

PUBLIC LIBRARY UNIONS:
BANE OR BOON?

Rashelle Schlessinger Karp

INTRODUCTION

In 1917 the first public library union was organized at the New York Public Library. This marked the first period of public library unionization in the United States. Until 1920, the number of unions in public libraries grew, as "economic forces generated by the World War were stimulating organization of workers in all fields" (Berelson, 1939, p. 492).

With the emergence of economic well-being in the 1920s, and consequent anti-union sentiment, unions began to decline. Out of the original five (at the Library of Congress, New York Public Library, Boston Public Library, Washington Public Library, and the Philadelphia Public Library), three were disbanded (New York Public Library, Boston Public Library and Philadelphia Public Library).

Advances in Library Administration and Organization, Volume 4, pages 25–54.
Copyright © 1985 by JAI Press Inc.
All rights of reproduction in any form reserved.
ISBN: 0-89232-566-6

"The next movement toward library unionization . . . did not come until 1934, but in the intervening 15 years . . . staff associations" engaged in protective actitivities (Berelson, 1939, p. 496). This "second period" (Guyton, 1975, p. 17) of library unionization lasted through the 1940s and was due in large part to librarians' efforts to counteract the economic effects of the depression.

Another factor linked to the development of unions during this period was the passage to the 1935 National Labor Relations Act, which gave workers in the private sector the legal right to "self-organization, and designation of representatives of their own choosing, for purposes of negotiating the terms and conditions of their employment or other mutual aid or protection" (National Labor Relations Act, 1977, Sec. 151). Although this Act excluded federal, state and local government employees, it was an important antecedent to similar legislation for public sector employees.

The relative prosperity of the 1950s accounted for another decrease in union activity, but by the 1960s several dormant unions had been reactivated and several new unions had emerged. This third period (which continues today) began as one of "ferment: radical antiwar activities occurred on the campuses from whence librarians came, . . . librarians and library students rose at the Atlantic City ALA Conference, the feminist movement developed, professional unions were becoming more acceptable, and teachers, nurses and doctors joined unions" (Biblo, 976, p. 423).

Federal legislation has also promoted unionization during this period. In 1962, President John F. Kennedy signed two Executive Orders in response to recommendations made by the Task Force on Employee–Management Relations in the Federal Service. Executive Order 10987 recognized that "the public interest requires . . . safeguards to protect employees against arbitrary or unjust adverse actions . . . [and that] the prompt reconsideration of protested administrative decisions to take adverse actions against employees will promote the efficiency of service" and improve employee–management relations (U.S. President, Executive Order 10987, p. 519).

Executive Order 10988 determined that "participation of employees in the formulation and implementation of personnel policies affecting them contributes to effective conduct of public business" and that "the efficient administration of the Government and the well-being of employees require that orderly and constructive relationships be maintained between employee organizations and management officials" (U.S. President, Executive Order 10988, p. 521). The order also gave federal employees the right to organize.

And in 1969, President Lyndon B. Johnson signed Executive Order 11491, which attempted to standardize the federal labor-management relations system and make it conform more closely to the system in place in the private sector (U.S. President, Executive Order 11491).

The reasons for unionization are numerous. However, it is generally agreed that "the decision to go union does not occur in a vacuum; it reflects perceptions ⟨of the employees⟩ that obviously diverge significantly" (Harris, 1977, p. 237) from those of the employers. A list of perceptions that can cause conflict includes:

1. Public librarians' dissatisfactions with opportunities for promotion within the library (Blake, 1972)
2. Public librarians' perceptions of a lack of opportunity for study and research on the job (Handsaker, 1969)
3. Salary levels ("In favor . . .," 1921; Starr, 1946; Tufts, 1964)
4. Public librarians' workload (Blake, 1972)
5. Working conditions ("Brooklyn . . .," 1967)
6. Lack of collegial feeling between administrators and employers (Brose, 1975)
7. Growth of technology and comcomitant depersonalization of the working environment, which may alienate employees and lead to concerns about job security, reassignments, and accountability (Weatherford, 1976; Bentley, 1978)
8. "External forces such as inflation, energy cost, and taxes which adversely affect the funding, purchasing power, and operating costs of public libraries" and "have a direct bearing on relationships between library employees and their administrators" (Viele, 1982, pp. 320–321)
9. Increases in the size and scale of library services which may limit the individual librarian's degree of autonomy (Golodner, 1967; Schlachter, 1976)

10. A perceived lack of participation in the library's decision-
making processes (Freeman, 1976)

Public librarians have formed small inhouse unions of their
own (called staff associations); they have affiliated with national
labor unions such as AFSCME (American Federation of State,
County, and Municipal Employees) or the AFL–CIO (American
Federation of Labor–Congress of Industrial Organizations); and
they have joined local and regional unions composed of different
occupational categories within several governmental levels (often
called municipal employee unions). The variety of unions with
which librarians have affliated is an interesting fact associated
with the profession's service orientation and the profession's
small size (Dolan, 1971; Boaz, 1971; Berry, 1975; Robb, 1975).
Whatever the justification, and however it is achieved, unionization is an important issue with which the profession of librarianship must deal.
The literature of librarianship presents debate regarding the
merits of unionization for librarianship. Much of the debate revolves around two major aspects of any profession: the preem-
inence of the profession as a whole (Phelps, 1946; Smith, 1937;
Mleyenek, 1970), and the subsequent level of professionalism of
its practitioners (Smith, 1968; Schlipf, 1975). This essay reviews
librarians' opinions about library unionization, and describes direct and related research regarding public library unionization.

LIBRARIANS' OPINIONS ABOUT LIBRARY
UNIONIZATION

Professionalism of Practitioners

A major area of concern regarding the unionization of librarians
is how unionization might affect the professionalism of practitioners within the field. Several major issues that must be discussed follow below.

The Artificial Adversary Relationship

"Librarians' faults are many, library trustees have but two—
everything we say, everything we do. Keeping this sage obser-

vation in mind, I venture to say librarians are better off by not unionizing" (Mayer, 1979, p. 242). Mayer's observations illustrate one of the major arguments advanced in the literature against library unionization: unions cause, and indeed, thrive on an artificial adversary bargaining relationship between employees and employers (Weatherford, 1976; Herman, 1978). They cause employees to "feel themselves natural enemies of their administrators . . ." ("Libraries . . .," 1967, p. 2118).

The very essence of the activity at the bargaining table is necessarily adversarial (Harris, 1976), because "there are inherent differences of interest between employees and those who employ them. Employers must make decisions about budgets, capital construction, staffing, and so forth. These matters will take precedence in their thinking. Employees, while interested in . . . the organization, are more immediately concerned with income, working conditions, and job security. Manager-professionals are managers first, as they must be. . . . Their decisions . . . therefore, will not be based on the same priorities that concern the professional employee." (Chamot, 1976, p. 491).

Seen another way, however, the "tension between the authority inherent in . . . the structure . . . of the organization and the authority of specialized knowledge and training . . ." has potential for positive effects (Knapp, 1973, p. 473). For example, it is valuable for the employer "to have the assurance that there are no forgotten groups in the organization . . . without ready channels of communication, . . . feeling that their problems are being ignored. . . . This is what collective bargaining is . . . the shaping of a constitutional basis for dealings with those who manage and those who are managed" (Tead, 1939, pp. 35–37).

It is further believed by union proponents that unionization is "emphatically . . . not an antiadministration movement. The union is simply, . . . trying to accomplish the very things for which the trustees and librarians have been striving. . . . If possible, it has made the members of the staff more sympathetic . . . with the administration through better appreciation of the difficulties which must be met" (Bowerman, 1919, p. 365). Thus, unions are seen to help administrators as well as nonadministrators by "working independently for higher wages and better working conditions; . . . increasing the involvement of the individual librarian in the problems of his library; . . . and providing a framework within which problems can be solved" (Mleyenek, 1969, p. 755).

Another aspect of the adversary issue concerns middle management, which is seen as a "grey area" between management and nonmanagement (Drum, 1978; Harrelson, 1972). Booth (1978) explains that the presence of unions tends to force middle management into one camp or another—administration or nonadministration. Because of this, middle management may be disadvantaged by divided responsibility toward the administrators whose policies they must implement and the employees whom they must supervise (Lewis, 1969). They may also be unhappy because of a lack of supervisory autonomy which is often caused by difficulties associated with classifying middle management into one or the other camp (Person, 1980).

Autonomy and Authority

A "qualified professional is supposed to be an *authority* on his subject, and an expert on its application" (this author's emphasis; Asheim, 1978, p. 233). He "subjects his decisions only to the review of colleagues and demands *autonomy* of judgment of his own performance" (this author's emphasis; Asheim, 1978, p. 230). Union opponents argue that unionization severely restricts the librarian's ability to be a professional by removing these elements from his control (Cottam, 1968). It is believed by many librarians that this removal of authority and autonomy diminishes the librarian's professional status. Others, however, agree with Falkoff (1937, p. 592) that unionization "cannot damage a professional status that is at best poorly defined, ineffectual and in many circles, not even recognized."

Another aspect of the autonomy/authority criterion is the need for the professional to be involved in his institution's decision-making processes. Dillon (1971) expresses the sentiments of many librarians when she states that participative management is a desirable managerial style because it allows for maximum autonomy of professionals within an institution. She believes that unfortunately, many administrators pay only "lip service" to the goal of participative management. In these cases, unionization is seen as a way of forcing administrators actually to use participative management, and so increase the professionalism of their employees. Conversely, DeGennaro (1972) and Shaughnessy (1977) maintain that unions are incompatible with participative management because of the adversary relationship that they foster between management and non-management. They further state that unions formalize negotiating procedures, a process which discourages, rather than encourages the librarian's individual freedom to participate in decision-making processes.

Commonality of Interest

An important concept of professionalism is that a "harmony of interest exists between professional staff and administrators. . . . It is argued that [since] these two professional groups share the same concern and interest in developing the profession; cooperation, rather than conflict, is expected to characterize their relationship. . . . If harmony . . . between managers and professional staff ⟨is an⟩ essential element in professionalism, . . . any force which appears disruptive would be viewed as . . . unprofessional" (Schlacter, 1976, p. 458). Conversely, Wagner (1975) points out that unions establish procedures for communication between managers and professional staff which are constructive rather than disruptive.

Looking at the commonality of interest question from a different viewpoint, some librarians claim that even if the union supports professional goals, the methods that it uses to achieve these goals are unprofessional (i.e., strikes). This may negate any professionalism that the union might possess (Hale, 1937; "Papers . . .," 1919; Ballard, 1982).

Other librarians question whether they "can even communicate with union people" ("Libraries . . .," 1967) since it is felt that there is no commonality of interest between the "rights and aspirations [of the professions] and those of industrial and commercial . . ." labor (Sherman, 1939, pp. 39–40). Those workers are linked to a single, specialized operation, vocation, or industry. Librarians are not so fettered because "theirs are trained intellects, developed skills, experienced judgments—portable, and transcending space and boundaries" (Sherman, 1939, p. 40).

Professional Goals

Kleingartner (1975, p. 16) identifed two types of goals which he labeled Level I and Level II goals. He defined Level I goals "as those relating to fairly short-run job and work rewards . . .

which include fundamental concerns of satisfactory wages or salaries, suitable working conditions, fair treatment, reasonable fringe benefits, and a measure of job security. Level II goals . . . [were] defined as the longer-run professional goals . . . not generally held by manual workers as realizable objectives. . . . These goals are seldom translated into concrete objectives except by professionals . . . [because] much of the substance . . . is encompassed in the concepts of autonomy [and] occupational integrity. . . ."

It is argued by union opponents that unions bargain only for Level I goals, and in fact are legally "limited to negotiating about wages, hours, and other terms and conditions of work" (Ballard, 1982, p. 506). Ballard (1982) divided the union's scope of negotiations into three categories: (1) mandatory (management cannot refuse to discuss these subjects); (2) illegal (topics that contravene the law); and (3) permissive (management may bargain about these, but is under no obligation to do so). Most "professional," or Level II, concerns are seen to fall into the permissive category. This led him to conclude that "since the legal power to force bargaining is totally lacking for permissive subjects, management typically refuses to discuss them" (Ballard, 1982, p. 506).

Preeminence of the Profession

A second major area of concern regarding the unionization of librarians is how unionization might affect the profession as a whole. Several major issues that must be discussed follow below.

Affiliating with Other Unions

Much of the debate concerning unionization revolves around the size of the profession's membership. Proponents argue that because the number of librarians is small, "only collectively can we as . . . librarians attain our goals" (Haro, 1968, p. 1554). This sentiment is echoed by Wasserman (1975, p. 29), who states that "only through a collective voice does any individual professional, public employee have any voice at all."

Union opponents agree that the power of individuals is based upon their ability to speak collectively. However, they also point out that the power of a collective group is commensurate with its size. Since librarians are a small profession, they are forced to join unions "made up of all types of members" in order to have an effective voice. Opponents claim that in doing this, librarians "lose their identity just by the large difference in their number as compared to the number of other members" (Dolan, 1971, pp. 228–229).

This loss of identity is compounded by the democratic structure of the union. "There is no place for . . . the development of the specific goals of any one profession. . . . The individual librarian, in a union, becomes a member of a heterogeneous group and pursues only employee welfare for the whole group" (Boaz, 1971, p. 106). Librarians thus find themselves in a union dominated by other occupational groups, where concerns unique to their profession are often overlooked or subordinated to the pressure of the dominant groups (Berry, 1975; Robb, 1975). As unions get larger, librarians may need to be protected from the "domination of the labor union, in which librarians [are] . . . a minority" (Hale, 1937, p. 588).

Another by-product of minority status is that a "union may disrupt library service by involving library employees in one of its external 'fighting issues' " (Robb, 1975, p. 359). These might include issues which are not only external to the profession of librarianship, but possibly external to the union itself such as a sympathy strike (Simonds, 1975).

The Strike

"To be effective . . . a union must have some sort of coercion. The traditional weapon has been the strike" (Post, 1969). Union opponents disagree. They point out that the power of a threatened strike is neutralized by the nature of librarianship because librarians "do not produce articles of tangible value. Communities support them not because they *must* but because they believe in them" (Hale, 1937, p. 588). "Unions get their power from their right to strike; professions get theirs from a unique ability to serve. Unions and professionals are at opposite ends of the spectrum" (Brenneman, 1975, p. 6). Instead of forcing employers to recognize librarians' worth, strikes may have the opposite effect of demonstrating that "library service is irrelevant" (Post,

1969, p. 476) because there will be little tangible effect on the public. "Public sympathy must be aroused to bring about increased recognition of the library and its potentialities; labor union methods which lean towards pressure and disturbance, rather than reason, education, and persuasion are not best calculated to succeed" (Hale, 1937, p. 588).

The small size of the profession is also cited as a major neutralizer of the strike threat. Discussing academic librarianship, Axford (1977, pp. 277–278) claims that "academic librarians are too small a group to affect significantly the normal operation of the university should they decide to walk off the job in a contract dispute."

Bureaucracy of Unions

Another major debate revolves around the bureaucratic nature of institutions. It is felt that union growth and its resultant bureaucracy has led to many effects:

1. Abuses of power that result in "sordid activities" of the union (Dolan, 1971, p. 230)
2. Regimentation within the union, which caused Goldstein (1968, p. 12) to remark, "it seems sad that librarians may be turning to unions at a time when many unions are suspected of no longer following liberal policies"
3. Formalization of promotion and tenure rules that may make it easier (through contract clauses concerning professionalism) for librarians to sustain their professional competency and positive identification with librarianship ("National . . .," 1981); conversely, this formalization may stifle "the growth of new talent" (Nyren, 1966, p. 5905; Trelles, 1972) and entrench incompetents (Berry, 1975, p. 245)
4. Formalization of work hours which prevent coercion of employees but which may also severely limit the employees' freedom to work nontraditional hours when desirable (Cottam, 1967)
5. Procedural rules which can either make the union incompatible "with social change and experiment" (Nyren, 1968, p. 4077), or provide it with the power to force administrators (who often resist) *to* change (Smith, 1970)

6. The political nature of the union, which may provide librarians with a political power base from which to defend intellectual freedom (Reiter, 1969); it might also move the work of the library from an "intellectual context into a political arena which subverts the primary intellectual traditions of the institution. . . ." (Michener, 1974, p. 20)

7. The superimposition of the union over the library, which may cause a significant increase in the amounts of time and money required to deal with nonlibrary activities (Berry, 1975; Garbarino, 1975); these new demands may decrease the professional's time to perform professional duties (Kirkpatrick, 1972, p. 196), or they could have the opposite effect of increasing time available for the performance of professional duties by relieving librarians of nonprofessional tasks for which they no longer have time (Mendlow, 1969)

It is also believed that unionization introduces a second power structure into "what may have been a unilateral decision-making hierarchy" (Oberg, 1976, p. 443). This is perceived as intruding upon professional prerogative (Scarich, 1975) by upsetting informal working relationships as it requires formalization of procedures. Conversely, introduction of a second power structure is also perceived as advancing professional prerogative because it prohibits arbitrary decision-making by library administrators who may restrict professional independence (Oberg, 1976).

Unions and Professional Associations

Many librarians echo the sentiments expressed by McDonough (1968, p. 874): "I am not against unions per se. I don't feel that unions, can, or will, exhibit . . . concern for the profession. . . ." It is further argued that the differences between labor unions which are predominantly concerned with employee welfare, and professional associations which are additionally concerned with the profession as a whole, make unions unnecessary and detrimental to the profession (Cottam, 1968). Conversely, Day (1973) argues that if the existence of a professional association is essential to a profession, then the existence of a union with its special powers is also esssential. The American Library Association (ALA) "does not support adequate salaries and working conditions, although librarians want this kind of activity, are willing to pay for it, and will turn to unions if it is not supplied by ALA . . ." ("Democratization . . .," 1970, p. 367). "Don't lament them [unions], for our own ⟨association's⟩ inactions and inabilities created them" (Hartnett, 1977, p. 20).

Throughout the years, the ALA has developed its position concerning unions. Citing obstacles that might be insurmountable were the ALA to become a union (Auld, 1969; Moulton, 1969), the ALA's official stance is that "library unions may not be able to contribute to the promotion of library service" (ALA Third Activities Committee, 1939a, p. 796). "The American Library Association can choose between two courses in regard to conditions of employment and salaries . . . either . . . such matters are not a proper subject of study by a professional organization" or they are (ALA Third Activities Committee, 1939b, p. 406). "ALA should be neither purely an educational organization nor an organization designed exclusively to benefit its members personally" ("New . . .," 1970, p. 239). ALA will thus work with organized labor (ALA Library Unions Round Table, 1941), but will remain an "association whose primary concern is with the aims, the mission, and the work of the profession" ("The new member . . .," 1965, p. 995). "As a national library organization of librarians, trustees, industries which serve library needs, and other concerned members, the ALA" ("The American Library Association and . . .," 1970)

recognizes the principle of collective bargaining as one of the methods of conducting labor-management relations used by private and public institutions. The Association affirms the right of eligible library employees to organize and bargain collectively with their employers, or to refrain from organizing and bargaining collectively, without fear of reprisal. . . . As a national education organization, the ALA will: 1) inform librarians, other library employees, library administrators, trustees, boards of education, and appropriate officials about collective bargaining trends, methods, and contracts; 2) assist librarians, other library employees, library administrators, trustees, boards of education, union organizations, and appropriate officials in gathering data and information to enable them to develop better employment patterns and contracts; 3) encourage and conduct educational programs to train librarians, other library employees, library administrators, trustees, boards of education and appropriate officials in collective bargaining, and in working effectively within contractual employment patterns; 4) encourage type-of-library divisions to develop guidelines and recommendations for their type of institution (Guy, 1982, p. 4).

Standards

"Organization of public library employees into strong and effective unions . . . will surely bring the standards of the profession to a much lower level than now exists" (Kennemer, 1939, p. 778). Librarians in 1983 are still repeating Henry's (1919, p. 284) warning, "Our people can unionize and change our standards from a profession to a trade." "If unionism comes into the library, then we will lower our standards, our morale, our self respect and our appeal to those we serve" (Ferguson, 1938, p. 526). Members of a profession need "no contract to tell [them] how long to work—⟨they⟩ will work until the job is done" (Kirkpatrick, 1972, p. 193).

Contrary to the belief that unions will bring about lower standards, proponents argue that higher quality library service is an eventual goal and a result of unionization's achievements for librarians ("Brooklyn Library . . .," 1967). These achievements "will enhance the attractiveness of librarianship as a profession, and hence attract more and better qualified people" (Brandwein, 1967, p. 510). The natural result of unionization's gains for librarians, especially higher salaries, will be the extension of library service ("Ask National . . .," 1939; American Library Association, 1941); greater prestige and higher standards for the profession (Davies, 1936); and higher valuation of the work done by librarians (Herbert, 1919).

Proponents of unions believe that "no matter how idealistic you may be, it's easier to be sure that you're doing something worthwhile if society recognizes the value of your work to the extent of paying a decent wage for it" (Thistlethwaite and Wycoff, 1936, p. 414). "Librarians and other professional[s] . . . have been content to live largely in insecurity and inadequately because they considered it undignified to press for higher wages. . . . [T]his servile attitude [has] contributed to the backwardness of their profession" (Speer, 1944, p. 101).

Service Orientation

Some opponents of unionization question the appropriateness of a union for public service employees such as public librarians. "Public libraries were not established for the benefit of a profit-making employer; nor for a job seeking employee class. They were founded for a consumer reading public and for no other reason. . . . Unions have one primary purpose—the constant improvement of the working conditions of the worker. . . . The [public] . . . takes second place or perhaps no place at all in their thinking. Without the weapon of collective bargaining . . . workers in profit-making industry would in some cases be helpless, at the mercy of unscrupulous profit-making employers. In libraries there is no parallel to such a situation" (Sherman, 1940, p. 406).

Tucker (1939, pp. 42–43) and more recently, Boaz (1971), counter the above arguments: "Public servants are coming to realize that they are not untrue to the public weal, when they align themselves with the rest of the labor movement to improve their own conditions and promote the welfare of their occupation. The American labor movement is the true representative of the hopes, aspirations, and interests of the great majority of our population, for it is the lever that has raised the American standard of living—the pride of the American people. Professionals are coming to realize that, far from holding aloof, it is their duty, in the progressive tradition, to ally themselves, through cooperation with the labor movement, with the public whose servants they are. Only by such cooperative effort can there be the proper advancement of public services."

RESEARCH ON LIBRARY UNIONIZATION

The paucity of research on public library unionization led Cottam (1968, p. 1341) to remark that "librarianship is not doing enough research on issues involved in unionization. ⟨It is⟩ only getting biased opinions." Although the current investigation is concerned with unionization for public librarians, selected research in the areas of academic and school librarianship has been included in this literature review. This related research has been selected for inclusion because of its value as a comparison to the field of public librarianship, and because of the contributions it has made to the general body of knowledge concerning unionization for librarianship.

Historical

In 1939 Berelson wrote the earliest study of collective bargaining in United States public libraries. His history covered the period of 1917–1939, and its stated purpose was "to outline the background material necessary for any appraisal of the desirability and value of library unionization . . ." (p. 470).

During the 1950s, Clopine (1951) and Spicer (1959) added further information to Berelson's study and updated it. Clopine developed a three-phase model to explain the evolution of public library unionization in the United States.

The first phase, according to Clopine, began shortly after World War I, when the economic forces created by the war were causing widespread organization of workers in many different fields. With the emergence of economic well-being in the 1920s, and concomitant antiunion sentiment, library unionism entered a second phase and declined rapidly. The third phase began in the 1930s as a result of the economic depression which characterized those years. During this period, and up to the present, unionism began to flourish once again. Among Clopine's major conclusions were (1) that unions usually develop in larger libraries supported by public funds; (2) that effective unions developed only in cities friendly to unionization and in libraries where good relations existed between the union and the library administration; (3) that the presence of staff associations did not prevent unionization; (4) that library unions played an increasingly important part in securing funds for libraries; and (5) that arguments for and against library unionization had not been resolved (1951, pp. 143–144).

In 1968 Goldstein collected information and position statements concerning unionism from 154 library directors in United States public, academic and government libraries with collections of 500,000 volumes or more. His unpublished seminar paper stated as its purpose "to set forth a history of library unionization in the United States from the inception of this activity until now, to note the current status of this phenomenon in individual libraries and to consider and comment on some aspects of the unionization of librarians, existing agreements, the terms of current contract and some of the details of current understandings between unions and libraries as well as the demands of unions" (p. 1). Goldstein's research was seriously flawed by an apparent lack of objectivity, a methodology that solicited opinions in open-ended format which made classification and comparison difficult, and an incomplete research design. However, his paper did provide detailed information about union contracts and the history

of unionization in specific libraries that was not easily accessible
elsewhere.

Survey

The American Library Association has done several surveys
of unionization in libraries, beginning in 1967, when the Library
Administration Division (LAD) surveyed adminstrators of 91
public libraries serving populations of 350,000 or more. The survey was largely descriptive of the kinds of collective bargaining
within the libraries and how their bargaining procedures worked.
When queried about their attitudes toward unions, 3 percent of
the respondents stated that they would encourage unionization
of library employees, 20 percent said they would discourage it,
68 percent were neutral, and 9 percent made no comment. It is
interesting to note that the administrators' attitudes on whether
unionization should be encouraged were not consistent with their
attitudes regarding recourse of library employees to collective
bargaining. On this question, 63 percent felt that professionals
and nonprofessionals should have recourse to collective bargaining, 64 percent felt that library employees should have the
right to affiliate with organized labor, and 11 percent said that
library employees should have the right to strike. Finally, 66 percent of the respondents "indicated a need for a full-scale survey
on labor in librarianship" to provide a guide for librarians "in
determining effective bargaining units and agencies at national
and local levels" (Gardiner, 1968, p. 975).

In 1968, the LAD sent a 10-item questionnaire to union stew-
ards and library directors of seven public libraries which had
union contracts. The questions focused on the reasons why library employers organize, changes that unionization has or will
have in libraries, who should be members in library unions, staff
associations as bargaining agents, the scope of collective bargaining, preparation for collective bargaining, and the legality of
collective bargaining (ALA, 1968). The published comments
echoed opinions already documented in the first part of this literature review.

Also in 1968, the ALA's Staff Organization Round Table
(SORT) surveyed 150 nonunionized SORT member libraries. The
purpose of the SORT study was to "find out something about

librarians' opinions of unionism in their profession" (ALA. Staff Organizations Round Table, 1969, p. 803). Of the 2185 respondents (including 39 percent professionals, 14 percent subprofessionals, and 46 percent nonprofessionals), 42 percent said the they would probably belong to a union if the library had a union; 48.8 percent said they would probably not belong to a union if the library had a union; and 8.3 percent were undecided. Ten percent of the responders thought it likely that their libraries would have a union within 5 years; 75.4 percent thought it unlikely that their libraries would have a union within 5 years; and 14.4 percent would not make any predictions. A high percentage of the respondents believed that unionization would improve salaries, but that it would make "little difference" in pension plans.

Several other surveys have been completed since unionization became a reality in public libraries. In 1949, Fitch surveyed administrators and librarians in five public library unions. She asked about union membership, union-management relations, and gains that the union had been able to make in the areas of salaries, insurance, pension plans, vacation allowances, and staff participation in decision-making. She concluded that unionization was beneficial for the librarians and administrators queried.

In 1952, Bryan wrote *The Public Librarian*. Her research was based upon the 1946 Public Library Inquiry (which was funded by the Carnegie Corporation through the Social Science Research Council). In her book Bryan reported the Public Library Inquiry's findings concerning public librarians' and administrators' attitudes toward staff associations and unions. Specifically, the study examined public librarians' and administrators' present and past memberships in staff associations and unions; their attitudes toward the desirability of one over the other; and their perceptions of gains achieved. The study found that one-fifth of the librarians had not formed opinions concerning library unionization, about one-fourth were opposed to it, and about one-fourth were doubtful of the value of library unionization. "Approximately [one-fifth] believe[d] sufficiently in the principle of unionization to join a labor union, while only 6% [were] willing to work actively toward unionization of the workers in their libraries" (Bryan, 1952, p. 275).

In 1967, the Massachusetts Library Association published its "Findings from a questionnaire survey on the impact and implications of the Massachussetts Collective Bargaining Law on public libraries." Hopkins (who conducted the survey reported that only 76 out of the 389 public library administrators who were sent questionnaires made comment. Over half of the respondents (43) stated that "collective bargaining had no application to their library because of their small size and lack of employee interest. . . . The remaining . . . administrative comments . . . were divided between lack of adequate knowledge and the relevance of the state library asssociation in this matter." Hopkins also registered disbelief that such large numbers of library administrators were truly neutral on such a "volatile issue" (1969, p. 3404).

Two other state library associations have examined the climate for public library unionization. In 1967, the Michigan Library Association found that a large group of librarians were favorable to the idea ("Special Committee . . .," 1967), and in 1970 the Ohio Library Association found that 42 percent of Ohio public librarians favored the proposition that the Ohio Library Association become the bargaining agent of library employees ("Beguiling Figures," 1970).

"The first reasonably analytical studies of library unionization did not occur until 1970, when Vignone compared attitudes of Pennsylvania library directors, library board members, and librarians . . ." (Guyton, 1975, p. 9). Vignone's stated purpose was to "determine, compare and describe the opinions and attitudes of three groups involved with public library service in Pennsylvania—library directors, librarians, and library board members—regarding collective bargaining in libraries. [Secondly, it concentrated] on the opinions and attitudes of the above three groups as they relate[d] to the provisions of [a constructed] model framework of collective bargaining procedures" (1970, p. 15).

Vignone's study concluded that library directors and librarians were more favorable toward collective bargaining than trustees. He also found that younger, better educated librarians were more favorable toward collective bargaining. Sex, level of experience, professional affiliation, and size of population served were found not to be related to attitudes about collective bargaining (p. 145).

Guyton (1975, p. 2) studied "the pattern of public library unionism from its inception to the present. The analyses focus[ed] on identifying factors that promote[d] or hinder[ed] unionization

among librarians and on developing theoretical statements concerning the emergence of library unions". His intent was to develop a theoretical model that would explain why some libraries
unionized and others did not.

Guyton surveyed public librarians in unionized and nonunionized Southern California libraries. He asked questions about librarians' degrees of satisfaction with (1) their salaries, (2) their
libraries' organization and administration, and (3) the intrinsic
satisfaction provided by their jobs. He also asked questions which
were designed to measure attitudes toward unionism in general.
Guyton was able to develop a composite of a "pro-union" librarian. The pro-union librarian seemed to be "younger, male,
earning a lower salary, better educated, and from lower social
origins" (p. 176). He also identified three environmental factors
which seemed to encourage unionization: (1) employment concentration, or bureaucratization that tends to create a "structural
barrier between administrators and librarians which inhibits their
degree of personal contact and communication"; (2) a legislative
climate which permits the formation of library unions; and (3)
an existing tradition of strong labor unions in the geographic area
(p. 177).

Finally, Guyton developed a three equation descriptive model
to explain that: (1) library unionization is a "function of the degree of opportunity consciousness and the nature of certain ex-
ogenous factors that promote or hinder unionization" (p. 177);
(2) bureaucratization is a function of employment concentration
or administrative policy; and (3) legislative climate, proximity to
organized employees, and the availability of unions, promote
unionization (pp. 177–180).

In 1971, Schlachter studied librarians from academic libraries
in seven midwestern states. She examined "the relationships between ⟨academic⟩ librarians' attitudes toward collective bargaining, strikes, and union membership . . . and selected personal,
educational, situational, and associational characteristics" (p. 1).
She also examined what kinds of representation academic librarians had experienced and what types of associations they
preferred to represent them. Schlachter concluded that the participants in her study preferred independent, local employee associations over traditional labor unions or professional associations (p. 353). She found that librarians in her sample most likely

to approve of unionism were young, male, single, and politically liberal. They also had had little supervisory experience, were recently employed at their present jobs, were members of professional associations, were dissatisfied with their salaries, and had had previous exposure to union membership (p. 353).

In 1973, Wyatt examined the "attitudes of three professional groups, academic librarians, library directors, and deans toward union organization and collective bargaining for academic librarians" (p. 1). Wyatt's sample was from academic libraries employing more than five librarians in eight Southeastern states.

Wyatt found that librarians were more favorable toward unionization than deans and library directors. He also found that the unfavorable attitudes of library directors and deans were closely aligned. He suggested that this phenomenon could be attributed to a "common administrative experience and outlook" (p. 90). It is interesting to note that Wyatt's (1973) findings concerning academic librarians differed from Vignone's (1970) earlier findings concerning public librarians. Wyatt found that academic library directors were closest to deans, or upper level administrators, in their attitudes toward unionization. However, Vignone found that public library directors were closest to librarians, or nonadministrators, in their attitudes toward unionization.

Wyatt also analyzed the relationship between selected personal aspects and attitudes toward collective bargaining; race, sex, prior union membership, professional association membership, type of institution and size of institution were not. Like Schlachter, Wyatt found that younger, lower salaried, less experienced librarians held more favorable attitudes toward unionization (p. 129). However, Wyatt found that married librarians, not single librarians (as Schlachter had found) held more favorable attitudes toward unionization (p. 105).

In 1980, Caynon studied the relationship between collective bargaining and the professional development of academic librarians in four-year public institutions of higher learning in the United States.

Caynon attempted to "determine the extent to which a group of librarians employed in institutions of higher education with collective bargaining for librarians and a group of librarians employed in institutions of higher education without collective bargaining for librarians [were] involved in a select group of [professional development] activities; and to determine if the extent of involvement in these activities by these two groups of librarians varie[d] significantly" (p. 7).

He examined the following professional development activities: (1) membership in and attendance at meetings of professional library associations; (2) membership in and attendance at meetings of nonprofessional library associations; (3) number of library and nonlibrary professional journals and books read; (4) participation in continuing education; and (5) publications authored.

Caynon's study concluded the "In general, employment in collective bargaining environments does not significantly affect the involvement of academic librarians in professional development activities. . . . Factors such as library position, professional experience, eduation, age, sex, and salary ha[ve] little or no effect upon whether academic librarians in one environment were more or less involved in the activities studied than were academic librarians in the other environment" (p. 165).

Also in 1980, Mika investigated "the effects of collective bargaining on librarians and libraries . . . in selected academic institutions of Pennsylvania" (p. 10). The librarians in Mika's sample were members of faculty collective bargaining units. He concluded that academic librarians' "interest in unionization was not perceived as an abandonment of professional status; rather unionization was seen as an alternative means to achieving faculty status. Unionization was also viewed as the vehicle which would provide the broad political base necessary for the negotiating of librarian concerns [even though] . . . the academic librarians were too small a group to effect the negotiations significantly . . . [and] librarian concerns were bargained away in favor of administrative concessions for the teaching faculty" (pp. 228–229). Mika also found that (1) librarians' status did not change after the establishment of collective bargaining; (2) few tangible benefits were gained by librarians at unionized institutions; and (3) only "active participation, visibility, and constant contact by librarians with bargaining agents will insure their attention to librarian concerns . . . [and] overcome [librarians'] minority status" in bargaining units (p. 230).

One other survey of academic librarians appeared in 1980. Peace "explored factors which appeared to cause academic librarians [in ARL libraries] to desire collective bargaining . . .

[and] examined how librarians' attitudes were translated into behavior at election time" (Abstract).

Peace identified two major problems in Schlachter's (1971) earlier study: (1) Schlachter's study had "a somewhat oversimplified design" because it "examined the impact of personal characteristics on an individual's attitude toward collective bargaining . . . [but] overlooked environmental and institutional factors" which were "critical in explaining attitude toward unionism"; and (2) "the set of personal characteristics she [Schlachter] introduced was too limited . . . [because] she ignored the impact of attitudinal characteristics" (Peace, 1980, p. 56).

Peace thought that other studies had suffered from the same problem of omitting "factors significantly related to collective bargaining" (p. 63).

Peace concluded that "the type of librarian most likely to hold a favorable attitude toward collective bargaining would be a young, male librarian who is politically liberal, has little supervisory experience, favors faculty status, distrusts university administrators, is pessimistic about the job market and has been exposed to a union" (p. 198).

The most recent research on public library unionization was completed by Lilore in 1982. Lilore examined the local union of public libraries by (1) examining "the internal relationships among the leaders and members" of local unions; (2) investigating the union's "external relationships with management"; and (3) analyzing labor union contracts (pp. 1–2).

Lilore's study took two years to complete, during which time she used four methodologies: "participant observation, survey, interview, and content analysis" (p. 14).

She concluded that:

1. "The labor management relationship is a dynamic one, moving on a continuum from accomodation to antagonism. The two groups basically have an adversarial association" (p. 60).

2. "The ⟨negotiating⟩ process as a whole . . . [is] ritualistic and traditional" (p. 115).

3. "Public library local unions have little bargaining power which makes them weak at the negotiation table" (p. 115).

4. The union's "preparatory internal negotiations are more heated and time consuming than . . . external negotiations with management" (p. 116).
5. "Conflict between professionals and nonprofessionals" in the same union is not a major area of internal disagreement within the local union (p. 221).

Although not directly related to this research, three other dissertations on unionization in librarianship should be mentioned. In 1975, Adams looked at differences in librarians' status in public academic libraries with and without collective bargaining. She discovered that librarians at institutions with collective bargaining had better status than librarians at institutions without collective bargaining, but that the better status was gained before collective bargaining appeared on the campus, not after. Cruzat (1976) examined how academic librarians fared as members of faculty collective bargaining and concluded that they did not fare well. Mosley (1980) examined the extent to which Florida public school library media specialists and their programs were mentioned in collective bargaining agreements, and whether the negotiation goals of the school library media specialists were similar to the teachers' goals. Mosley found that school library media programs were mentioned "infrequently" in negotiated agreements for Florida school districts and that teachers and school library media specialists did not share similar negotiation goals (1980, pp. iii–v).

CONCLUSIONS

Thus far research has not provided a clear consensus regarding the benefits of unionization for public librarians. There is a great need for further research on the issue. Some of the questions that must be answered include:

• How does unionization affect librarians' professionalism and their opinions of librarianship *as* a profession?
• How does unionization affect the public's perceptions of librarians as professionals?

- Has unionization increased librarians' salaries, job security, and fringe benefits?
- Are some types of unions more suitable than others for librarians?
- Can evaluative measures of professionalism and fulfillment of service standards be included in union contracts?
- Should such measures be included in union contracts?
- Can a union adequately represent the interests of librarians?

These questions and others like them must be carefully examined if we are to make knowledgeable decisions concerning the desirability of unions for public librarians, and ultimately for the advancement of the entire profession.

REFERENCES

Adams, M. L. L. "A comparison of librarians' status between academic institutions with and without faculty collective bargaining units (Doctoral dissertation, University of Missouri)." *Dissertation Abstracts International,* 36 (1975):7069A. (University Microfilms No. 76–11,474)

The American Library Association and library collective bargaining (position paper adopted by the Library Administration Division Board of Directors, January 21, 1970). In American Library Association, *Position statements and policies and procedures.* Chicago: American Library Association, 1970.

American Library Association. "Collective Bargaining: Questions and Answers." *ALA Bulletin,* 62 (1968):1385–1390.

American Library Association. "Library Unions Round Table. Proceedings at ALA Conference 1940–1942." *ALA Bulletin,* 35 (1941):119–123.

American Library Association. Staff Organizations Round Table Survey. "Opinions on Collective Bargaining." *ALA Bulletin,* 63 (1969):803–809.

American Library Association. Statement on Professional Ethics 1981. *American Libraries,* 12 (1981):335.

American Library Association. Third Activities Committee. "Final Report." *ALA Bulletin,* 33 (1939a):782–805.

American Library Association. Third Activities Committee. "Tentative report." *ALA Bulletin,* 33 (1939b):352–453.

Asheim, L. "Librarians as Professionals." *Library Trends,* 27 (1978):225-257.

Ask National Drive to Organize Librarians, *ALA Bulletin,* 33 (1939):700–701.

Auld, L. W. S. "ALA and Collective Bargaining." *ALA Bulletin,* 63 (1969):96–97.

Axford, H. W. "The Three Faces of Eve: Or the Identity of Academic Librarianship: A Symposium." *Journal of Academic Librarianship,* 2 (1977):276–285.

Ballard, T. H. "Public Library Unions—the Fantasy and the Reality." *Library Journal,* 13 (1982):506–509.

Beguiling Figures. *Ohio Library Association Bulletin,* (October 1970):20–22.

Bentley, S. "Collective Bargaining and Faculty Status." *Journal of Academic Librarianship,* 4 (1978):75–81.

Berelson, B. "Library Unionization." *Library Quarterly,* 9 (1939):477–510.

Berry, J. "Unions in Libraries: Another Side." *Library Journal,* 100 (1975):245.

Biblarz, D. et. al. Professional Associations and Unions: Future Impact of Today's Decisions." *College and Research Libraries,* 36 (1975):121–128.

Biblo, H. "Librarians and Trade Unionism: A Prologue." *Library Trends,* 25 (1976):423–434.

Blake, F. M. "Labor Unions and Librarians: A Rejoinder." *California Librarian,* 3 (1972):46–49.

Boaz, M. Labor unions and libraries. *California Librarian,* 32 (April/July, 1971):104–108.

Boissanas, C. "ALA and Professionalism: Heading in the Right Direction?" *American Libraries,* 3 (1972):972–979.

Booth, R. "There Ain't No Middle." *Illinois Libraries,* 60 (1978):577–578.

Bowerman, G. F. "Unionism and the Library Profession." *Library Journal,* 44 (1919):364–366.

Brandwein, L. et al. "Unions and Professionalism." *Library Journal,* 92 (1967):508–510.

Brenneman, H. W. "The Species Professio." *Michigan Librarian,* (Fall 1975):4–6.

"Brooklyn Library Union to Seek Better Service." *Library Journal,* 92 (1967):38–40.

Brose, F. K. "Collective Bargaining: Can We Adjust To It?" *California Librarian,* 36 (1975):37–47.

Bryan, A. I. *The public librarian: a report of the public library inquiry.* New York: Columbia University Press, 1952.

Butler, P. "Librarianship as a Profession." *Library Quarterly,* 21 (1951):235–247.

Caynon, W. A., Jr. A study of the relationship between collective bargaining environments and the professional development of academic librarians. (Doctoral dissertation, Indiana University, 1980) *Dissertation Abstracts International,* 41, 838A. (University Microfilms No. 8020018)

Chamot, D. "The Effect of Collective Bargaining on the Employee Management Relationship." *Library Trends,* 25 (1976):489–496.

Clopine, J. "A History of Library Unions in the United States." Unpublished Master's thesis, Catholic University of America, 1951.

"College Librarians Hear Union Debate." *Library Journal,* 94 (1969):17.

Cottam, K. "Unionization for the Unhappy." *Library Journal,* 92 (1967): 510.

Cottam, K. "Struggle for Allegiance [letter]." *ALA Bulletin,* 62 (1968):1340–1342.

Cottam, K. "Unionization is not Inevitable." *Library Journal,* 93 (1968):4105–4106.

Cruzat, G. M. S. Collective Bargaining in academic Librarianship. (Doctoral dissertation, Wayne State University, 1976) *Dissertation Abstracts International*, 37, 6818A. (University Microfilms Order No. 77–9385)

Davies, L. "Librarianship and Organization." *Wilson Bulletin for Librarians*, 10 (1936):543–544.

Day, A. "Unattainable?" *New Library World*, 74 (1973):145–146.

DeGennaro, R. "Participative Management or Unionization?" *College and Research Libraries*, 33 (1972):173–174.

"Democratization of the Association: Interim Report." *American Libraries*, (1970):366–379.

Dillon, J. Unite! *Synergy*, (Summer, 1971):21–22.

Dolan, J. "Librarians Unite!" *Minnesota Libraries*, 23 (1971):228–232.

Downey, L. J. "What else is There?" *Focus on Indiana Libraries*, 23 (1969): 573–575.

Drum, K. "The Grey Area." *Illinois Libraries*, 60 (1978):573–575.

Executive Order No. 10,987, 3 C.F.R. (1962).

Executive Order No. 10,988, 3 C.F.R. (1962).

Executive Order No. 11,491, 3 C.F.R. (1969).

Falkoff, B. "Should Librarians, Unionize? Part II—The Librarian and the Closed Shop." *Library Journal*, 62 (1937):590–593.

Ferguson, M. J. "The Library Crosses the Bridge." *Library Journal* 63 (1938):523–526.

Fitch, V. K. "Organized Labor in the Library." *Library Journal*, 74 (1949):1069–1071.

Fitzgibbons, S. Ethics. In R. Wedgeworth (Ed.), *ALA Yearbook, 1977*. Chicago: American Library Association, 1977.

Flexner, A. *Medical education in the United States and Canada: a report.* (Bulletin no. 4). New York: Carnegie Foundation for the Advancement of Teaching, 1910.

Freeman, D. "Professionalism Trends toward Unionism." *California Librarian*, 37 (1976):18–25.

Garbarino, J. W., Kemerer, F. R., and Baldridge, J. V. *Unions on campus: a national study of the consequences of faculty bargaining.* San Francisco: Jossey-Bass, 1975.

Gardiner, G. L. "Collective Bargaining: Some Questions Asked." *ALA Bulletin*, 62 (1968):973–976.

Goldstein, M. S. *Collective bargaining in the field of librarianship.* Unpublished manuscript, 1968. (Available from author: 5123 Post Rd. New York, New York, 10471)

Golodner, J. "Librarian and the Union." *Wilson Library Bulletin*, 42 (1967):387–390.

Guy, J. *Unionization and collective bargaining: TIP Kit #1.* Chicago: American Library Association, 1982.

Guyton, T. L. *Unionization: the viewpoint of librarians.* Chicago: American Library Association, 1975.

Hale, R. "Should Librarians Unionize? Part I – The Librarian and the Open Shop." *Library Journal*, 62 (1937);:587–589.

Handsaker, M. "Professional Negotiations and Collective Bargaining by Public Employees." *New Jersey Libraries,* (Fall 1969):19–24.

Hanks, G. and Schmidt, C. J. An alternative model of a profession for librarians. *College and Research Libraries,* 36 (1975):175–187.

Haro, R. P. "A Call to the Meek." *Library Journal,* 93 (1968):1553–1554.

Harrelson, L. E. Library Unions: Some Issues." *Oklahoma Librarian,* (October 1972):11–13; 35.

Harris, P. "Advice for the New Trustee Negotiator." *Wilson Library Bulletin,* 52 (1977);237–240.

Harris, P. "Tough-minded Trustee Bargaining: Always Legal; Often Appropriate." *Public Library Trustee,* (March 1976):3.

Hartnett, T. "Troubleshooters View the Growth of Unionism." *Connecticut Libraries,* (1977):18–20.

Henderson, J. "Consulting in Union–management Relations." *Library Trends,* 28 (1980):411–424.

Henry, W. E. "Living Salaries for Good Service." *Library Journal,* 44 (1919):282–284.

Herbert, C. W. "Recruiting a Training Class: An Experience and some Reflections Thereon." *Library Journal,* 44 (1919):107–108.

Herman, S. J. "Staff Organization Round Table." *Library of Congress Information Bulletin,* 37 (1978):443–445.

Hopkins, J. S. "Unions in Libraries." *Library Journal,* 94 (1969):3403–3407.

"In Favor of Library Workers Unions." *Library Journal,* 46 (1921):360.

Kennemer, J. D. "Drive to Organize Librarians." *ALA Bulletin,* 33 (1939):777–778.

Kirkpatrick, O. "The Professional Librarian as Unionist." In E. J. Josey (Ed.), *What black librarians are saying.* Metuchen, N.J.: Scarecrow Press, 1972.

Kleingartner, A. and Kennelly, J. R. Employee relations in libraries: the current scene. In F. A. Schlipf (Ed.), *Collective bargaining in libraries.* Champaign–Urbana: University of Illinois Graduate School of Library Science, 1975.

Knapp, P. B. The library as a complex organization: implications for library education. In C. Rawski (Ed.), *Toward a theory of librarianship.* Metuchen, NJ: Scarecrow Press, 1973.

Lewis, R. "A New Dimension in Library Administration: Negotiating a Union Contract." *ALA Bulletin,* 63 (1969):455–464.

"Libraries and Labor Unions." *Library Journal,* 92 (1967):2115–2121.

Lilore, D. M. The Local Union of Public Librarians. (Doctoral dissertation, Columbia University, 1982). *Dissertation Abstracts International,* 43 1333A. (University Microfilms No. 8222430)

McDonough, R. H. "An Inaugural Address." *ALA Bulletin,* 62 (1968):873–878.

Massachusetts Library Association. Public Library Administration Division. *Findings from a questionnaire survey on the impact and implications of the Massachusetts collective bargaining law on public libraries.* Boston: The Association, May 15, 1967.

Mayer, Albert. "Unions, Plus or Minus? *Wilson Library Bulletin,* 54 (1979):242–243.

Mendlow, S. "Teachers of Library Unite!" *Library Journal,* 94 (1969):2537–2538.

Michener, R. E. "Unions and Libraries: The Spheres of Intellect and Politics." *Southeastern Librarian,* 23 (1974):15–25.

Mika, J. J. Patterns of collective bargaining: an investigation into the development and consequences of faculty collective bargaining, unit certification and contract negotiation on professional librarians in academic institutions of Pennsylvania. (Doctoral dissertation, University of Pittsburgh, 1980). *Dissertation Abstracts International,* 41, 2339A. (University Microfilms No. 8028066)

Mleyenek, D. G. "Professional Unions." *California Librarian,* 31 (1970):110–118.

Mleyenek, D. G. "Unions, What's in it for Administrators? *Wilson Library Bulletin,* 43 (1969):752–755.

Mosley, M. M., Jr. An investigation of the perceptions of Florida school library media specialists and teacher negotiation team members toward specific collective bargaining proposals. (Doctoral dissertation, The Florida State University, 1980) *Dissertation Abstracts International,* 41, 3768A (University Microfilms No. 8104868).

Moulton, D. "ALA as Union." *ALA Bulletin,* 63 (1969):431–432.

National Labor Relations Act. 152, 28 U.S. Code (1977).

"National Librarians Association Seeks Links with Unions." *Library Journal,* 106 (1981):2076.

"New directions for ALA: Interim Report." *American Libraries,* 1 (1970):238–241.

"The New Member and the ALA." *ALA Bulletin,* 59 (1965):995–1001.

Nyren, K. "Editorial: The Brooklyn Gambit." *Library Journal,* 91 (1966):5905.

Nyren, K. "The Union Question." *Library Journal,* 93 (1968):4077.

Oberg, M., Blackburn, M., and Dible, J. "Unionization: Costs and benefits to the Individual and the Library." *Library Trends,* 25 (1976):423–433.

Orman, O. C. "550 Librarians Speak." *Wilson Library Bulletin,* 14 (1940):572–573; 587.

Papers and proceedings of the forty-first annual meeting of the ALA held at Asbury Park, New Jersey, June 23–27, 1919. *Bulletin of the ALA,* 13 (1919):375–386.

Peace, N. E. Attitudes of professional librarians in selected research libraries toward collective bargaining. (Doctoral dissertation, Columbia University, 1980) *Dissertation Abstracts International,* 43, 1334A. (University Microfilms No. DA8222463)

Person, R. J. Middle managers in academic and public libraries: managerial role concepts. (Doctoral dissertation, University of Michigan, 1980) *Dissertation Abstracts International,* 41, 1820A. (University Microfilms No. 8025745)

Phelps, O. W. "Organizations of Employees, with Especial Reference to Library Personnel." *Library Quarterly,* 16 (1946):20–34.

Post, J. "Go-slow Strike." *Library Journal,* 94 (1969):475–476.

Reiter, C. J. "Laying it on the Line." *Library Journal,* 94 (1969):1953–1954.

Robb, P. P. "Changing Loyalties: Effects of Unionization on Communication Patterns in Libraries." *Canadian Library Journal,* 32 (1975):357–367.

Roscoe, S. "Unions and School Librarians." *School Library Journal,* 22 (1976):44.

Scarich, K. "Libraries and Unions: Two Sides." *Connecticut Libraries,* No. 4, (1975):10–11.

Schlachter, G. A. Professional librarians attitudes toward professional and employee associations as revealed by academic librarians in seven midwestern states (volumes I and II) (Doctoral dissertation, University of Minnesota, 1971). *Dissertation Abstracts International, 32,* 4643A. (University Microfilms No. 7205575)

Schlachter, G. A. "Professionalism v. Unionism." *Library Trends,* 25 (1976):451–474.

Schlipf, F. A. (Ed.). *Collective bargaining in libraries. Proceedings of a conference.* Champaign–Urbana: University of Illinois Graduate School of Library Science, 1975.

Shaughnessy, T. W. "Participative Management, Collective Bargaining, and Professionalism." *College and Research Libraries,* 38 (1977):140–146.

Sherman, C. "The Unionization of the Professions as one Librarian Sees It."*ALA Bulletin,* 30 (1939):38–41.

Sherman, C. "Unfinished business of T.A.C." *Library Journal,* 65 (1940):406–407.

Simonds, M. J. "Work Attitudes and Union Membership." *College and Research Libraries,* 36 (1975):136–142.

Smith, E. "Librarians and Unions: the Berkeley Experience." *Library Journal,* 93 (1968):717–720.

Smith, E. "Librarians' Organizations as Change Agents." *Focus on Indiana Libraries,* 24 (1970):178–181.

Smith, S. W. In union—is there strength? *Wilson Bulletin for Libraries,* 11 (1937):310–311.

"Special Committee to Study the Implications of Public Act 379." *Michigan Librarian,* (October, 1967):28.

Speer, L. "Professional Worker in Organized Labor." *Pacific Northwest Library Association Quarterly,* 8 (1944):100–101.

Spicer, E. *Trade unions in libraries: the experience in the United States* (Canadian Library Association occasional paper, No. 23) Ottawa: Canadian Library Association, 1959.

Starr, M. "Librarians and Labor." *Library Journal,* 71 (1946):383–387.

Tead, R. "Professional Workers and Unionism." *Special Libraries,* 30 (1939):35–38.

Thistlethwaite, D. M. and Wycoff, D. Post conference conversations. *Wilson Bulletin for Libraries* 10 (1936):367–371; 414–416.

Trelles, O. M. "Law Libraries and Unions." *Law Library Journal,* 65 (1972):158–180.

Tucker, W. P. "Unionization for Special Librarians," *Special Libraries,* 30 (1939):41–45.

Tufts, A. "The Librarian and the Union." *British Columbia Library Quarterly,* (April, 1964):7–9.

Viele, G. B. Problems and strategies for collective bargaining in public libraries. In C. R. McClure & A. R. Samuels (Eds.), *Strategies for library administration: concepts and approaches*. Littleton, Colorado: Libraries Unlimited, 1982.

Vignone, J. A. An inquiry into the opinions and attitudes of public librarians, library directors, and library board members concerning collective bargaining procedures for public library employees in Pennsylvania (Doctoral dissertation, University Pittsburgh, 1970). *Dissertation Abstracts International, 31*, 6081A. (University Microfilms No. 7113224)

Wagner, M. Grievances. In F. A. Schlipf (Ed.), *Collective bargaining in libraries*. Champaign–Urbana: University of Illinois Graduate School of Library Science, 1975.

Wasserman, D. Unionization of library personnel: where we stand today. In F. A. Schipf (Ed.), *Collective bargaining in libraries*. Champaign–Urbana: University of Illinois Graduate School of Library Science, 1975.

Weatherford, J. W. *Collective bargaining and the academic librarian*. Metuchen, N. J.: Scarecrow Press, 1976.

Williamson, C. C. *Training for library service: a report prepared for the Carnegie Corporation of New York*. New York: D. B. Updike, the Merrymount Press, 1923.

Wyatt, J. F. A study of the attitudes of academic librarians, library directors, and academic deans in colleges and universities of 8 southeastern states toward union organization and collective bargaining for academic librarians. (Doctoral dissertation, The Florida State University, 1973). *Dissertation Abstracts International, 34*, 6676A. (University Microfilm No. 7409503).

SATISFACTION WITH LIBRARY SYSTEMS

Larry N. Osborne

BACKGROUND

The search for satisfaction with library automation systems has historically been a part of the planning process, which in turn, has been primarily devoted to: identifying the specific uses to which the system will be put, specifying exactly how the system must perform in these uses, selecting the system which will provide the best cost performance ratio, implementing the system so as to maximize the chance of success, and then monitoring the performance so that it is possible to determine the extent to which the system accomplishes the functions for which it was created.

In other words, planning is designed to ensure success in a given installation, where success is defined as an installation where the actual performance of the system meets or exceeds

Advances in Library Administration and Organization, Volume 4, pages 55–75.
Copyright © 1985 by JAI Press Inc.
All rights of reproduction in any form reserved.
ISBN: 0-89232-566-6

its specifications. This definition assumes that if specifications are written reflecting the actual needs of the library, then the system will resolve the problem at hand; if, for example, a backlog has developed in the cataloging department and it has been determined that, assuming no increase in staff or decrease in acquisitions, a throughput of x books per hour is required to allow same-week cataloging, then specifications as to cataloging database size, response time, keystrokes per item, and so on, may be written for submission to vendors. The assumption is that if the delivered system meets the specifications, and that the specifications reflect the reality of the needs, then the system is a success. Unfortunately, a system may be a success in these terms, yet both staff and management may be dissatisfied with it and backlog may actually increase.

The key to this phenomenon is a failure to understand the difference between success and satisfaction. Success is a quantifiable concept directly related to the planning process; satisfaction is a feeling people have. There is little evidence to link the two concepts to a single antecedent.

The Concept of Satisfaction

Satisfaction is a slippery concept, and librarians, especially those who attempt to emphasize the "science" in library science, are justifiably leery of slippery concepts. It is much easier to count the number of keystrokes necessary to retrieve a given record, or even the number of minutes required to answer the "average" reference question, than to determine whether the reference librarian is satisfied with the retrieval system or the cataloger with the bibliographic database. Nonetheless, satisfaction is, or should be, an important concept for librarians on the line, for library managers, and for system vendors.

Effects of Dissatisfaction

It is enticing at this point to define satisfaction in detail, but probably it is more useful to proceed with an intuitive feeling for what satisfaction is, and move directly to what Czepiel and Rosenberg have termed the "so what?" question. While answering this question, they point out that dissatisfaction produces such observable phenomenon as "angry consumers, worried managers, protesting consumer advocates, and rule-making government officials" (Czepiel and Rosenberg, 1977).

Less obvious but in the long run equally important results were investigated by Day et al. (1981). He began by listing nine possible responses by consumers to unsatisfactory experiences: (1) doing nothing; (2) personally boycotting the product class; (3) personally boycotting the brand; (4) personnally boycotting the seller; (5) privately complaining to associates; (6) seeking redress from the seller; (7) seeking redress from the manufacturer; (8) seeking redress through a third party, such as consumer groups or the courts; (9) complaining publicly for reasons other than redress (e.g., to influence future actions of retailers and/or manufacturers; to warn the public; or just "to get it off my chest"). Day notes that "those consumers who elect to take some action as a result of an unsatisfactory experience tend to take actions of a personal or private nature" (Day et al., 1981).

In a library setting, possible examples of such private actions might be, on an individual level, complaining to co-workers about the automated system without making specific complaints to management; and at the management level, writing disillusioned articles on automation. There may be more dramatic results. In a recent study by the present writer (Osborne, 1983) satisfaction with automated systems at all levels (operator, department head, and chief executive officers) was found to be lowest in newly implemented systems and highest in systems over three years old. It was difficult to hypothesize a cause for this effect until, in the course of a number of site visits, the question was put to system users. Almost all immediately gave the same explanation: the dissatisfied employees had quit, transferred to other positions, or been fired.

While automation may occasionally be perceived by management as an opportunity to dispose of undesirable workers, it is doubtful that such is generally the case. The perception that dissatisfaction with computerization leads to common and large-scale dislocation of workers must be viewed with concern, and should be the subject of future study.

In the absence of such study one may conjecture that the non-complaining behavior defined above would be equivalent to the form of staff response familiar to managers as passive resistance or guerrilla warfare. Such behavior does not need to be intentional or malicious to be disruptive. In one discussion of the problem (Koogler et al., 1981) four possible effects of stress-induced resistance to a systems change were listed: (1) the proposed system change may fail to meet objectives; (2) the proposed change may have deleterious effects on work productivity; (3) the proposed change may cause a deterioration in human relations; (4) the adverse effects of a systems change may continue long after the system has either been implemented or discarded. It is a well-accepted concept that workers can make even the best system appear to be a failure if they wish. In a somewhat hysterical report "On Being Automated" (Downing, 1983), behavior of this type is chronicled:

> [T]hey developed their own ways of showing their dissatisfaction. They discovered the code necessary for bringing the system down for maintenance, and then gained 10 or 15 minutes time before it could be brought up again. They discovered that strong magnets can erase computer tape and even though it meant that they had to do the work over again, they derived some interim satisfaction from knowing that the bank's deadlines weren't being met and the customers weren't satisfied. And occasionally, when things got bad, the word would go down the line and 110 operators would all stand up at the same time and go to the toilet. But when things really became unbearable, they would "forget" to key in their personal reference code which was necessary for their productivity count, and would proceed to key in obscenities which would come out on the printout to the customer, and because the work was standardized, no one knew who had done it.

Such behavior as a response to a perceived threat goes back at least as far as Frederick Taylor's early experiences in attempting to force machine-shop employees to operate their lathes in a manifestly more quick and efficient manner. While there are many factors which might lead to such actions (see for example Fine's 1979 study), certainly library managers cannot afford to risk a system's success because of a failure to attempt to ensure user satisfaction.

Obviously, in a field as rife with networks, usergroups, associations, publications, and informal contacts among what in commercial fields would be competitors, system vendors must be concerned with the effects of this "noncomplaining" behavior on their product's sales. In a study by a major soft drink producer

(Coca-Cola Company, 1981), it was estimated that less than 1 percent of customer complaints were received by corporate headquarters, the rest being handled by local agencies or not being made "officially" at all. The pyramidal structure of Coca-Cola is analogous to that of a vendor such as OCLC, which may have many levels of intermediaries between the home office in Dublin, Ohio, and the cataloger with a perceived problem.

The report also notes that those who don't complain feel that business will be unresponsive, or that they don't know who to complain to. In any case the results of dissatisfaction were shown to be either decreased purchases (44.4 percent) or refusal to buy the producer's product at all (30.9 percent).

The Definition of Satisfaction

Assuming that the importance of satisfaction to library administrators and system vendors has been shown, the question of its definition may now be considered. As a first step let us discuss what satisfaction in this concept does not mean.

Most library studies involving satisfaction have prefixed the word with either "job" or "user." The former usually refers to the attitude an individual has toward librarianship in general and toward his/her current position in particular, while the latter is usually a study of requests for information filled or unfilled and/ or the relevance of information supplied to the user. Both areas of study are useful and important to librarianship, but neither definition of satisfaction is synonymous with that used here.

Before proceeding to what satisfaction does mean here, the word"user" in the preceding paragraph requires additional clarification. In general in library literature, users are the end-users of library services—what public librarians refer to as patrons and special librarians call clients. When discussing automated systems, however, this definition breaks down: the users of an on-line cataloging system are not the library's clients, but its catalogers. Even when the public actually touches the equipment, as in public-access catalogs, the client is a user of the library's services, in this case through one of its terminals, and not of its computer. This concept may be clarified by examining other automated professions, such as hospitals, and banks. A patient in a hospital who has a CAT scan is not a user of the computer system, except in a very narrow sense; even a bank customer who makes a withdrawal at an automatic teller is a bank customer and not a computer system user. In both these cases, and in the sense in which the term is used here, the patient or customer is a user of the institution (bank or hospital) which is the system user. The doctors, hospital administrators, tellers and bankers are the users and customers. They may be completely satisfied even if their clients or patients are not. Eventually, of course, we hope the needs and satisfactions of the two groups will be in agreement, but each must be considered independently. When the words "user" or "customers" are used here, they refer to the librarians or libraries who select and use the systems, not to the end users, clients, or patrons of the library's services.

As to the definition of satisfaction itself, two approaches suggest themselves, which may be called the psychological definition and the marketing definition.

The psychological, or scientific, approach to a definition stresses measurable changes in a laboratory setting. Most recently this approach has defined satisfaction as the degree to which the actual outcome of a product or situation matches the expectations an individual held at the outset. "Satisfaction, then, can be seen as an additive combination of the expectation level and the resulting disconfirmation" (Oliver, 1980). To measure satisfaction with a meal, using this definition, one would first ask the diner what he/she expected, serve the meal and then ask how good it was. Satisfaction would be the extent to which the two measures agreed. Obviously this approach can best be employed in an experimental setting with lowcost items. An experimenter can attempt to manipulate expectations for a ballpoint pen, give the subject an actual pen, obtain a rating of the pen's perceived quality, and thus measure the degree of satisfaction with the pen. It is more difficult to imagine such an approach being taken with an automobile or computer system. In the cases where measurements of relatively expensive merchandise has been attempted, for example with videotape recorders (Churchill and Surprenant, 1982), a large element of fantasy or role playing must be introduced.

The marketing approach also defines satisfaction as the degree to which pre- and postpurchase expectations agree; but, since it deals with actual purchases, expectations cannot be manipulated in the classical pre-test/post-test manner. Instead, marketing studies generally are predicated on only a single contact with the consumer, in which he/she is asked what expectations existed going into the purchase and whether the product met those expectations. In the meal example above, a marketing researcher would approach diners leaving a restaurant and ask, "was the food better or worse than you expected." Actual questions are usually variations of "Are you satisfied," "Would you buy this product again," "Would you recommend this product to others," or "What is your opinion of this product?"

Both definitions are based on the concept of confirmation of expectations. The opposite of confirmation, disconfirmation, is assumed to be a determinate of dissatisfaction in both cases. The former (pretest/posttest) case is a measure of inferred disconfirmation, while the latter (the single test case) is a measure of perceived disconfirmation. While the two concepts are distinct theoretically, correlation between them in studies varies from .54 to .89. (Swan and Trawick, 1981)

At least two scales have been developed for single-contact determinations of satisfaction. One is a general measure of consumer discontent (Lundstrom and Lamont, 1976). According to them, this scale, a Likert-type, with six intervals (ranging from "strongly agree" to "strongly disagree") is useful in studying "consumer behavior involving preferences for product classes, brands, retail outlets, etc." The scale uses questions derived from consumer literature, such as *Consumer Reports,* as its basis.

The other scale (Westbrook, 1980) is a single item scale, also of the Likert-type, which essentially asks a consumer to rate his/her feelings about the product or services on a scale from "delighted" to "terrible." It is based on the work of Andrews and Withey, (1976) and has been tested for durable goods and banking services. Westbrook claims that this approach allows more gradation of response, improves definition of response at the positive end of the scale, and is less demanding for respondents.

The Theoretical Base for Satisfaction Studies

Ultimately all satisfaction studies must either be dependent upon, or a reaction to, *A Theory of Cognitive Dissonance* (Festinger, 1957). In this seminal work Festinger theorized that if an individual is led to expect a certain outcome (e.g., that the Jap-

anese will win World War II, or that a computer system will
make his/her work easier and better) then, if the reality of the
situation is that the expectation is not met (the Japanese lose,
or the computer system doesn't work all that well), he/she will
act in some way which will serve to reduce the strength of the
dissonance perceived. While Festinger listed 12 ways in which
this might be accomplished, ranging from increasing the perception of the actual outcome's attractiveness (believing that the
computer system performs better than it actually does) to as-
sociating with others who suffer from the same dissonance (as
in the case of Japanese-Americans who asked to be sent to Japan
at the end of the war), marketing applications have emphasized
the first possibility.

Application of this theory in a marketing context results in
vendors making extremely glowing statements concerning their
products. In a computer example vendors would claim that their
system will solve all of a customer's problems; never break down;
cost practically nothing; and so on. When the system fails to live
up to its advertising, the dissonance reduction model would predict that the perception of quality felt by the buyers would actually increase as they tried to reduce the dissonance between
their expectations and reality. They would, in the end, be more
satisfied than if a truly objective presentation had been made in
the first place. While such an extreme example appears absurd,
reflection results in the realization that much product promotion
is based on a tacit acceptance of the dissonance reduction theory's validity. This theory has been explored in terms of product
satisfaction (Olshavsky and Miller, 1972) and job performance
(Cottrell, 1967), among other areas.

The opposite possibility, that overselling would result in customer backlash when the product turns out to be of lesser worth,
is generally referred to as disconfirmation theory. Studies in the
1970s by Olshavsky and Miller (1972); Anderson (1973); and
Oliver (1977) have tended to show that when expectations are
disconfirmed (for example: computer system doesn't live up to
the vendor's claims) satisfaction with the product is decreased.
Positive disconfirmation, the case where reality is better than
expectations, produces even more satisfaction than the neutral
case. System vendors who advertised on the basis of disconfirmation would intentionally understate their product's capabilities
with the expectation that customers would discover for them-

selves how great it really is, and their satisfaction would be even higher than if the system was presented objectively. There are obvious problems in actually behaving in such a fashion, but assuming the validity of disconfirmation theory system, vendors would have to be very careful not to overstate their system's good points and thus invite disconfirmation. Support for this theory has come from studies of both products (Oliver, 1977) and performance (Weaver and Brickman, 1974).

One of the delights of studying marketing is that the two most commonly accepted theories of satisfaction determination start with the same inputs and predict opposite results. As might be expected with such closely related theories, several attempts have been made to show underlying unity (Anderson, 1973; Cardozo, 1965). There are also several alternative theories of satisfaction causation: degree of effort needed to obtain the product (Allen, et. al., 1977); apparent freedom of choice (Reibenstein, Youngblood and Fromkin, 1975); and anxiety (Oshikawa, 1972). Summaries of these and other possible determinants may be found in Westbrook's "Interpersonal Affective Influences on Consumer Satisfaction with Products" (1980) and Churchill and Surprenant's "An Investigation Into the Determinants of Customer Satisfaction" (1982). Despite the existence of alternative and additional theories of satisfaction and of refinements on their basic concepts, dissonance and disconfirmation appear to be the most widely accepted models, with disconfirmation slowly displacing dissonance as the more popular paradigm.

THE MANAGEMENT CONTEXT

The importance of the same quantities called "satisfaction" in marketing studies has not gone unnoticed by management science writers. Generally the question of worker acceptance of a new system is considered a part of the implementation phase of the project development cycle. Little seems to have been written on manipulating longterm precursors of satisfaction.

Nonlibrary Systems

Libraries were not the first organizations to be automated, hence the problems which have only recently blossomed in our field were faced earlier in commercial automation projects. As long ago as the 1950s it was obvious that serious employee issues needed to be dealt with. In one study of a power-and-light company (Mann and Williams, 1960) automation had been accompanied by departmental reorganization and personnel transfer, as well as by increased integration of worker inputs and outputs. It was also accompanied by a breakdown of many of the usual communication paths. This study is particularly interesting because the company accepted a responsibility to reassign, and retrain if necessary, all of its regular employees. The resulting problems included maintenance of high morale in the changing environment, and a decrease in interdepartmental communications in the postplanning stages. Supervisors were faced with a staff who suddenly realized that the change would not generally be accompanied by promotion, as well as by workers who were really not suited to the new environment but were to be, according to policy, retained. Individuals were forced to confront a changed work environment where their old skills and company loyalty were not sufficient to ensure advancement. The project was a success: "The new system is permitting a reduction in cost and is sufficiently flexible to encompass future expansion." However, it is also noted, "The final effect on the individual members of the organization is still to be learned." No connection was made between the individual experiences of the employees and the overall success of the project.

In a subsequent report (Mann and Williams, 1962) they reported that more employees felt top management was not interested in them than had reported such beliefs before the changeover. More felt that the company was more interested in costs than people, and more employees said that their future looked worse after than immediately before the change.

More recent discussions have settled on the implementation phase of a project as the proper place to discuss employee reactions. As one recent report (Lee and Steinberg, 1980) states, "While a substantial amount of effort has been put into the development of manufacturing systems, the track record in terms of successful implementation is distressingly poor." They go on to list three commonly given reasons for implementation failure: technical (inappropriate and/or incorrect design); organizational (political); and people resisting change (lack of education or inattention to the way an organization works, or the irrational nature of people). Then they make a particularly cogent remark after relating two "horror stories": "This is fun! We can look at those who have failed and laugh at how dumb they must have been and at those who succeeded and marvel at how smart they were. We must, however, aim at more than that. . . ." They identify several factors which contribute to a system's success or lack of success: characteristics of the company management; psychological characteristics of the users; characteristics of collaboration between users and systems groups; characteristics of the project; characteristics of the project team and their approach; and characteristics of the project solution itself. It may be noted that how well the system works is only one of the factors listed.

In another discussion, this time of implementation failures (Guimaraes, 1981), four suggestions which might have prevented disaster were given: (1) require different requirements assurance strategies for different subsystems; (2) develop a satisfactory user suppport base; (3) expand management support for the system beyond budget allocation (e.g., "more effort demonstrating the advantages of the system"; and (4) a training program. Of the four suggestions, only one (the first) deals with what the system actually does.

Finally, after identifying stress-related resistance to change as a significant cause of implementation failure, Koogler, Collins, and Clancy (1981) cite six strategies to reduce this resistance. These may be summarized as follows: (1) collect sufficient relevant information; (2) establish and publicize how bad the current system is; (3) show how much better the new one will be; (4) ensure communication between all levels and types of employees; (5) provide employees with support and promote the new system; and (6) encourage participation in all phases of the change. Three of these (strategies 2, 3, and 5) are clearly marketing techniques based on satisfaction studies, and strategies 4 and 6 may fall into this category. Clearly, employees are seen as being consumers of the new system by a management which is trying to "sell" it to them, just as management is seen as customers by outside vendors.

Library Implementations

When libraries first began to seriously consider computerization as a means of better (or cheaper) service, they sought ways to ensure that they did not waste money, in other words, to guarantee success. A number of conferences in the late 1960s and early 1970s dealt with automation and the best way to make use of the electronic tools which were then becoming available. In one of the first, the 1965/66 Special Libraries Association meeting, many of the topics which later became standard considerations were discussed (Special Libraries Association, n.d.). Problem definition; systems analysis; identification of alternative solutions; flowcharting; selection of the best solution; exact specification of objectives for the new system; and the requirement for publishing the results were all mentioned. Several pitfalls to automation were also listed, including (1) underrating the cost of the installation, (2) allowing too little time for implementation, (3) setting improper goals, (4) selecting the wrong applications to automate, (5) making incomplete analyses, and (6) not keeping employees informed.

Automation was also the subject of a preconference institute at the 1967 American Libraries Association meeting (see ALA, 1969). Once again, in discussions on planning, understanding the current system through analysis and flowcharting was emphasized, along with endorsement of the hiring of special staff to aid in automation.

Other early prescriptions for library automation, selected arbitrarily, include Markuson's *Guidelines for Library Automation* (System Development Corporation, 1972) one of the earliest comprehensive works. While slanted toward federal libraries, her techniques were widely adopted. She included the requirement for a needs assessment; a survey of current resources; evaluation of budget suitability; study of the experience of others; systems analysis; and implementation as necessary parts of an automation project.

By 1975 Swihart and Hefley had listed 10 expectations for a computer system: (1) Provide the library staff with more information than is presently available with manual and visible records. (2) Be easy for the staff and public to use without extensive training in computer techniques or extensive changes in library principles. (3) Be reasonably economical. (4) Provide service to all functions in the library which can be automated. (5) Be modular and flexible enough for universal application without substantial redesign. (6) Provide a simple method of updating computer records. (7) Be designed so that processing and clerical decisions can be made by computer whenever possible, rather than manually. (8) Be able to exchange data with other libraries. (9) Be capable of operating in both centralized and decentralized modes. (10) Be limited to standard equipment generally available in computer centers and not require any unusual or special machinery.

The state of the art in the mid-1970s may be demonstrated by citing the management-level issues identified by Hayes and Becker (1974). These were (1) determining objectives, (2) preparing plans for achieving the objectives, (3) authorizing and controlling the required work, (4) monitoring and evaluating progress, (5) identifying alternative corrective actions as problems develop, and (6) informing staff of the effects upon them.

The list of papers and presentations giving advice to librarians faced by automation could go on and on, but in nearly all cases if the staff is mentioned as an important part of automation it is in the context of training them to handle the new system.

The situation has not changed in recent years. In describing the responsibility of management to develop systems which truly meet the immediate and long range needs of the library, Grosch (1979) identifies the tasks as "ensuring (a) that the system is installed, (b) that it is within budget in both its development and operations costs, and (c) that it performs as required."

Probably the most cited recent work on the practical aspects of library automation is *Choosing an Automated Library System* (Matthews, 1980). One measure of the increasing commonness of automation over a short period of time might be to compare the sense of adventure implied in Markuson's title, *Guidelines for Library Automation,* with the assumption of the commonplace expressed by *Choosing an Automated Library System.* Matthews, as might be expected of a person who is probably the foremost automation consultant in the United States, is conservative in his rules for automation. He restates most of the steps listed in the preceding studies and adds a post-implementation evaluation. Such a step is essential to determine if an implementation is successful, since, by definition, success is the degree to which a system meets the goals specified in the planning stages. As to ensuring staff acceptance, he states, "Unlike ducks and water, people do not take naturally to computer systems.

People, both staff and patrons, must be properly introduced to how computers work—and how computers do not work. They often must be cajoled into using the computer and seeing the ways the computer can help them in their work." To training and informing the staff we must apparently add, cajoling them.

The most recent major work on automation, Sager's *Public Library Administrator's Planning Guide to Automation* (1983), exhorts the library to follow ALA's *Planning Process for Public Libraries* (Palmour et al., 1980). Following the spirit of this document Sager specifies that "those who will be directly affected" be a part of the planning process. Such a role is important to ensuring satisfaction.

Effect of the Planning Process on Satisfaction

There appears to be little evidence linking the planning process to satisfaction with automated systems. In a recent study by the writer (Osborne, 1983), the planning process accounted for less than 10 percent of reported satisfaction. Indeed, few of the libraries had followed the generic planning process to any great extent. Of the eight steps in the process, the mean number of steps respondents were aware of their library having completed was 3.22. Other items with little correlation with reported satisfaction included the respondent's postion within the library hierarchy (clerical operators were no more or less satisfied than chief executive officers); type of library; perceived cost of the system; and the number of vendors contacted prior to system selection. One item examined is of particular interest to practicing librarians. There appeared to be no correlation between the system vendor and the degree of satisfaction felt by respondents. No single vendor was associated with a high satisfaction level, and no vendor, with the exception of Cincinnati Electronics, which was in the process of withdrawing from the market at the time the study was conducted, had a significantly higher dissatisfaction rate than any other. The general level of satisfaction was found to be fairly high; the mean satisfaction score for all respondents was 4.786 on a scale of 1 to 6. This may be cause for some rejoicing, or it may be the professional equivalent of the results of the traditional user (patron) studies, as summarized by Sager (1982). "More than 500 surveys were located in the literature, and one thing stood out in all of these surveys. The user was almost always well satisfied with the service received from his or her local library. That was true even if the institution was substandard and delivering wretched service in the opinion of the library's governance and staff."

Other factors which were not associated with satisfaction included many of the demographic variables: sex; age; length of time the respondent had worked in the profession; and whether the individual had been on the staff of the library prior to system implementation. This noncorrelation is in general agreement with studies of resistance to technology, such as Fine's 1979 report.

These are all negative findings. If many of the obvious candidates are not associated with satisfaction, librarians must ask what factors do seem to contribute to a feeling of satisfaction with automated systems.

In the study referred to above, this writer did establish several items which seemed to be associated with satisfaction. Not surprisingly, in light of the many marketing studies reviewed above, disconfirmation of expectations with the system was the largest contributor of those studied, accounting for at least 19 percent, and in some situations (systems less than one-year old, for example) over 50 percent of variance in satisfaction.

Other factors which were not associated with satisfaction included many of the demographic variables: sex; age; length of time the respondent had worked in the profession; and whether the individual had been on the staff of the library prior to system implementation. This noncorrelation is in general agreement with studies of resistance to technology, such as Fine's 1979 report. more satisfactory than those sold by nonlibrarians); the age of the system (older systems were judged more satisfactory); and the degree to which the respondent felt he or she was involved in the planning process.

PRACTICAL APPLICATIONS

Such investigations may be interesting, but they remain sterile unless they can be applied by field librarians. What can we learn from such studies?

First, we are forced to accept that satisfaction is important.

If we are system vendors, satisfaction on the part of customers is important; if we are library managers, employee satisfaction with the systems is of equal importance. If satisfaction is not achieved, customers will find subtle ways to make the system not work. It is not sufficient for a system to perform as planned. It must be perceived by the users as satisfactory.

Second, we cannot rely on the planning process as described in the numerous articles and books on the subject, no matter how well applied, to automatically produce employee satisfaction. While a feeling of participation in the process is associated with satisfaction, the process per se has little effect. This is the reason why Sager's committee was cited as a step in the right direction. Satisfaction, however, is a personal feeling; there is no indication that particpation by proxy is sufficient to promote satisfaction. Management must find a way to make all employees feel that they were intimately involved in the process.

Note that this is not, in any sense, a criticism of the planning process, or a claim that it is unimportant. Rather, it is a recognition that the planning process is designed to ensure that a system will meet the objectively determined needs of the library, not to ensure that that fact is appreciated by the staff.

In the same way, a governmental agency or system headquarters must avoid giving subordinate agencies the impression that a system is being imposed upon them, but bring them into the initial investigation and continue their subordinate's involvement through the decision-making process.

But the largest implication of recent marketing studies is that we have accepted the wrong paradigm of satisfaction genesis. The literature is filled with complaints about what, out of politeness, must be called over-optimistic reports: "Almost universally, library mechanization projects have started out with overly ambitious aims. . . .[T]he development schedules of library mechanization projects have depended on overly optimistic rates of progress, rates that simply were not met . . . and library mechanization projects have reported overly inflated claims of success" (Hayes and Becker, 1970). Or "computing is characterized by a promoter's bias. The bias is manifest in reports that, inter alia: (1) focus on success of a single system in a single jurisdiction, (2) tend to discuss impacts in a future-oriented verb tense . . ., (3) infrequently examine automated tasks that are evaluated as failures or major disappointments. and (4) examine the cost of EDP, financial and human, in a perfunctory manner and imply (with impressionistic evidence or none at all), that costs surely are outweighed by payoffs'' (Dansinger, 1977).

The tacit acceptance of the cognitive dissonance model is shown at all levels of library automation. It is illustrated when vendors make overenthusiastic sales presentations with the assumption that their customers won't mind too much when the truth hits them, when librarians make overly positive reports in the literature, and when managers who must whip up enthusiasm among future users of a system overstate its good points and cover up the inevitable glitches.

Such actions may be tactically expedient, but may backfire strategically. They constitute a dangerous shortcut.

For librarians this means that during the planning stages care must be taken not to imply that the system will accomplish more than is likely. This would be easier, of course, if, as Sager recommends, the actual users of the system are consulted early in the planning process. However, if only a staff representative is on the planning committee, management must see that true two-way communication takes place. If, for example, "wish lists" are solicited from line personnel, care must be taken not to imply that all wishes will come true.

Integrated systems and modules (such as a circulation system), which are expected to be eventually dovetailed, present a special problem. By definition they must satisfy a broad spectrum of users who often have conflicting expectations and needs. Under such circumstances it may be impossible for any system to live up to the expectations of all users. Special care must be taken in such cases to avoid excessive expectations and, hence, eventual disconfirmation. Equally thorny is the problem of expanding an existing system. Often the initial sale of the system was made on the basis of only a small portion of the expected final operation. This provides a sort of potential satisfaction time bomb. Naturally, the tendency is to implement the "best" part of the system first. If expectations for the remainder of the system are based on the showcase subsystem, disconfirmation is almost certain.

The lesson for vendors is equally clear. If the company's good name or repeat sales are considered valuable, take care that users don't expect more than the product can deliver. Vendors are doubly affected by disconfirmation of expectations. To a certain extent they can—through their advertising, responses to requests for proposals, and sales staffs—control the amount of disconfirmation customers will experience with their products. This may serve to affect indirectly the satisfaction management feels toward their systems. They cannot normally exercise the same control over the disconfirmation felt by the actual users of their systems. The gatekeepers to these people are the library management who may purposely or inadvertently oversell the system to their subordinates. Such overselling should be of direct concern to the vendors since it may lead to disconfirmation of expectations for the delivered system and thus to dissatisfaction being felt by the people who actually operate the system—and who can make a system they don't like look bad.

To overcome this problem vendors must educate library management in marketing techniques; must offer to speak directly to line personnel; and must monitor the way their products are being presented to eventual operators.

Finally, they should employ librarians to sell to libraries. It is unclear whether they present the product better than nonlibrarians, or whether they know what product to sell, or if there is some other reason; but individuals who know that their sales representative is a librarian tend to exhibit greater satisfaction with their systems than those who deal with nonlibrarians or don't know the professional background of their salespersons.

CONCLUSION

Systems are purchased to perform specific functions, not to provide satisfaction for library employees. Nonetheless, staff satisfaction can influence the success of the system and customer satisfaction is fundamental to the business success of the vendor. It seems only proper that this satisfaction be encouraged, especially when the major encouragement needed is the truth when known, and restraint, when reality must be conjectured.

Nor is such action manipulative. Instead, it serves to remove the impediments to satisfaction which might otherwise interfere with the apprehension of reality. It is the essence of communication.

It is true that additional investigation is called for, especially in the areas of the effect that the use of an outside consultant may have on satisfaction; the reasons behind the increasing satisfaction felt with older systems; and the way satisfaction changes as single-purpose systems are expanded or replaced with integrated systems. Also needed is a good investigation of the relationship between success of a system and satisfaction with it, since some recent evidence (Churchill and Surprenant, 1982) suggests that, at least for durable goods, neither initial expectations nor disconfirmation was as important in determining satisfaction as the product's actual performance. Such an investigation must await the availability of data on the level of success achieved by implemented systems, which is, in turn, dependent on the gathering of baseline data in preimplementation stages and adequate evaluation of implemented systems.

One intriguing possibility is that people who are faced with the necessity to automate, but are reluctant to do so, may actually engage in an internal marketing effort, literally selling themselves on the idea. If this is the case, yet another layer of expectation and potential disconfirmation may have to be unravelled.

Nonetheless, library managers and system vendors must take advantage of data and models which do exist. At the present time, this data suggest that no one can afford to ignore the effect that satisfaction or dissatisfaction can have on a product, an institution, or an individual.

REFERENCES

Allen, Bruce H., et. al. "Bargaining Process as a Determinant of Post-Purchase Satisfaction." *Journal of Applied Psychology* 62 (August 1977):487.

American Library Association. Preconference Institute on Library Automation, San Francisco, 1967. *Library Automation: A State of the Art Review.* Chicago: American Library Association, 1969.

Anderson, Ralph E. "Consumer Dissatisfaction: The Effect of Disconfirmation on Perceived Product Performance." *Journal of Marketing Research* 10 (February 1973):38.

Andrews, Frank M. and Stephen B. Withey. "Social Implications of Well Being." New York: Plenum, 1976.

Cardozo, Richard A. "An Experimental Study of Customer Effort, Expectation, and Satisfaction," *Journal of Marketing Research* 2 (August 1965):244.

Churchill, Gilbert A, and Carol Surprenant. "An Investigation into the Determinants of Customer Satisfaction." *Journal of Marketing Research* 19 (November 1982):491.

Cottrell, Nickolas B. "The Effect of Dissonance Between Expected and Observed Performanaces Upon Task Proficiency and Self-Estimates of Task Proficiency." *Journal of Sociological Research* 72 (August 1982):275.

Coca-Cola Company. *Measuring the Grapevine—Consumer Response and Word-of-Mouth.* Atlanta: Coca-Cola Company, 1981.

Czepiel, John A. and Larry J. Rosenberg. "The Study of Consumer Satisfaction: Addressing the 'So What' Question." In *Conceptualization and Measurement of Consumer Satisfaction and Dissatisfaction.* Cambridge, MA: Marketing Science Institute, 1977.

Dansinger, James N. "Computers, Local Governments and the Litany of EDP." *Public Administration Review* 37 (January/February 1977):28.

Day, Ralph L., et al. "The Hidden Agenda of Consumer Complaining." *Journal of Marketing* 57 (Fall 1981):86.

Downing, Hazel. "On Being Automated." *ASLIB Proceedings* 35 (January 1983):338.

Festinger, Leon A. *A Theory of Cognitive Dissonance.* Stanford, CA: Stanford University Press, 1957.

Fine, Sara. *Resistance to Technological Innovation in Libraries.* Final Report, Part II, Results of the Study. Washington, DC: Department of Health, Education, and Welfare, 1979.

Grosch, Audrey N. *Minicomputers in Libraries, 1979–1980.* White Plains, NY: Knowledge Industry Publications, 1979.

Guimaraes, Tor. "Understanding Implementation Failure." *Journal of Systems Management* 31 (March 1981):12.

Hayes, Robert M. and Joseph Becker. *Handbook of Data Processing for Libraries.* New York: Wiley, 1970.

Hayes, Robert M, and Joseph Becker. *Handbook of Data Processing for Libraries.* 2d ed. Los Angeles: Melville, 1974.

Koogler, Paul, Frank Collins, and Donald K. Clancy. "The New System Arrives." *Journal of Systems Management* 32 (November 1981):32.

Lee, William B. and Earle Steinberg. "Making Implementation a Success or Failure." *Journal of Systems Management* 31 (April 1980):19.

Lundstrom, William J. and Laurance M. LaMont. "The Development of a Rating Scale to Measure Consumer Dissatisfaction." *Journal of Marketing Research* 13 (November 1976):373.

Mann, Floyd C. and Lawrence K. Williams. "Observations of the Dynamics of a Change to Electronic Data-Processing Equipment." *Administrative Science Quarterly* 5 (1960):217.

Mann, Floyd C. and Lawrence K. Williams. "Some Effects of the Changing Work Environment in the Office." *Journal of Social Issues* 18 (1962):90.

Matthews, Joseph R. *Choosing an Automated Library System.* Chicago: ALA, 1980.

Oliver, Richard L. "Effect of Expectations and Disconfirmation on Postexposure Product Evaluations." *Journal of Applied Psychology* 62 (August 1977):480.

Oliver, Richard L. "A Cognitive Model of the Antecedents and Consequences of Satisfaction Decisions." *Journal of Marketing Research* 17 (November 1980):460.

Olshavsky, Richard W. and John A. Miller. "Consumer Expectations, Product Performance, and Perceived Product Quality." *Journal of Marketing Research* 9 (February 1972):19.

Osborne, Larry N. *Predictors of Satisfaction with Automated Circulation Systems.* Doctoral Dissertation. Pittsburgh, PA: University of Pittsburgh, Graduate School of Library and Information Science, 1983.

Oshikawa, Sadaomi. "The Measurement of Cognitive Dissonance: Some Experimental Findings." *Journal of Marketing* 36 (January 1972):64.

Palmour, Vernon E., Marcia C. Bellassai, and Nancy V. DeWath. *A Planning Process for Public Libraries.* Chicago: ALA, 1980.

Reibenstein, David J., Stuart A. Youngblood, and Howard L. Fromkin. "Number of Choices and Perceived Decision Freedom as a Determinant of Satisfaction and Consumer Behavior." *Journal of Applied Psychology* 60 (August 1975):434.

Sager, Donald J. "After the Planning is Over: Implementing Computerization." *Show-Me Libraries* 34 (December 1982):11.

Sager, Donald J. *Public Library Administrators Planning Guide to Automation.* Dublin, OH: OCLC, 1983.

Special Libraries Association. *Initiating a Library Automation Program.* Washington, DC: Special Libraries Association, Washington, DC Chapter, n.d.

Swan, John E. and I. Frederick Trawick. "Disconfirmation of Expectations and Satisfaction With a Retail Service." *Journal of Retailing* 57 (Fall 1981):49.

Swihart, Stanley J. and Beryl F. Hefley. *Computer Systems in the Library.* Los Angeles: Melville, 1975.

System Development Corporation. *Guidelines for Library Automation; a handbook for Federal and Other Libraries* by Barbara Evans Markuson [and others] Santa Monica, Calif. [1972]

Weaver, Donald and Philip Brickman. "Expectancy, Feedback, and Disconfirmation as Dependent Factors in Outcome Satisfaction." *Journal of Psychology and Social Psychology* 130 (December 1974):420.

Westbrook, Robert A. "A Rating Scale for Measuring Product/Service Satisfaction." *Journal of Marketing* 44 (Fall 1980):68.

BUDGETING AND FINANCIAL PLANNING FOR LIBRARIES

Michael E.D. Koenig and Deidre C. Stam

INTRODUCTION

This paper will attempt to be both a review of the literature of budgeting and financial planning in the context of libraries and information centers and a review of some of the basic concepts behind budgeting and financial planning. There are two aspects of financial planning and analysis that are intimately related to budgeting but that are beyond the scope of this review: one is long-range and strategic planning; the other is costing and cost analysis. The former has recently been reviewed in this journal (Koenig and Kerson, 1983), and the latter is scheduled for a review article in the near future.

Advances in Library Administration and Organization, Volume 4, pages 77–110.
Copyright © 1985 by JAI Press Inc.
All rights of reproduction in any form reserved.
ISBN: 0-89232-566-6

Budgets and Long-Range and Strategic Planning

The techniques and procedures of budgeting are in fact intimately related to the techniques and procedures of long range and strategic planning. Both deal with futurity—the question of how we should deploy resources in the future and to what end. Budgeting conventionally connotes the near future, the next year or two, and long-range planning connotes the medium and even the more distant future, but the two functions overlap considerably. The two should be an iterative and interactive recycling process with the deliberations and conclusions of long range planning feeding into the budgeting process. This point was emphasized in the previous review of strategic and long range planning that appeared in *Advances in Library Administration and Organization*.

The ramifications of this relationship is that at least as a planning procedure, budgeting must be thought of as a program based procedure. The essence of long range and strategic planning is to focus on what is to be accomplished, why and how, and this translates directly into a program budget, and from the program budget can be derived a line item budget, if that is administratively required.

This relationship between long-range and strategic planning and budgeting is one of the reasons for the increased emphasis upon program budgeting. Another interrelated reason is the profound impact of technological change upon libraries and information centers. The technology upon which libraries and information centers are based is changing with Moore's law rapidity— Moore's law being the observation that the number of elements that can be integrated into one chip is doubling every two years. Similarly the number of online databases is doubling every 2.3 years, the capability of fiber optics, every 1.5 years, etc. (Koenig, 1984). This is a far cry from the 24 years doubling period of traditional printing technology upon which traditional information services are built. This "sea change" has had many profound effects upon the field, but one of the most major changes has been the creation of the necessity for long-range and strategic planning. We can no longer easily predict the technology and the capability of the technology that will face us across the planning horizon. The difficulty of such planning has already led to the creation of an RLIN system that was designed to operate in a fashion that is now, only a few years later, economically and technologically inappropriate. Clearly the system would have been designed differently if the future, just the relatively short-term future, had been perceived more accurately.

In summary, the result of this rapidity of technological change is to force great emphasis upon planning, for at the same time that the rate of change of technology makes planning more different, it also makes it more important. The wealth of technology provides a choice of options that simply was not available before. This choice in turn forces a focus upon what is to be accomplished and why, and this in turn leads inevitably toward a programmatic emphasis in planning and budgeting. The options are now so many that they can no longer be taken for granted; they must be explicated, compared, and chosen.

Budgeting and Costing

The relationship between budgeting and costing is a very basic one. As library budgeting becomes more programmatically oriented, the relationship inevitably becomes more important. Program budgeting inherently requires the allocation of cost to the individual programs, that is to the outputs, and is therefore a process of cost accounting as well as a mechanism for budgeting.

Inclusion of a review of the literature of cost accounting and cost analysis is beyond the scope of this review, but it is intended that it be the subject of a subsequent review.

In passing, it should be mentioned that, to a large degree because of the increased emphasis upon budgeting analysis, there has been a corresponding increase in attention to costing and cost analysis in library and information operations.

Of particular interest is the publication by the American Library Association of a guide specifically on the subject of accounting for libraries and other not-for-profit organizations (Smith, 1983), although the emphasis is more upon external reporting than upon cost analysis and internal decision making.

A TAXONOMY OF BUDGETING METHODS

A budget is a quantitative expression of a plan of action and an aid to coordination and implementation. It serves, in the words of Horngren (1972, p. 121), as the "best practical approximation to a formal model of the total organization: its inputs, and its outputs."

The creation of a budget falls into the sphere of managerial, or cost, accounting. Managerial accounting, which relates costs to activities, differs from financial accounting, which records the use of funds. This distinction is seldom made clear in the literature of library budgeting, and it is a very important distinction.

Managerial accounting is undertaken for *internal* reporting in order to facilitate the planning and control of routine operations, to formulate policies, and to make nonroutine decisions, and plan for future actions. Because this kind of accounting focuses upon costs, it is commonly called "cost"accounting, a term which underplays its planning function.

Budgeting is one function of managerial accounting. Just as managerial accounting is an inexact science, involving extensive educated guesswork, so budgetng is a speculative and imprecise activity. The forms and processes of budgeting vary greatly from one institution to another, and from decade to decade. While budgeting has always taken place in libraries, this activity has been the subject of greatly increased attention in the literature during the past dozen years. In that span, one finds mention in the library field of budgeting methods devised in the private and governmental sectors. Each of these methods emphasizes slightly different aspects of institutional operations. While the methods do address overlapping concern, they seem to fall into two basic categories: those emphasizing *inputs* (funds), and those dealing with *outputs* (programs and services).

Recent lists of budgeting methods for libraries emphasize six systems. These are: line-item or incremental budgets, and formula methods, which emphasize funds; performance budgeting; program budgeting; planning–programming budgeting system (PPBS); and zero-based budgeting (ZBB), which emphasize outputs. The latter two are in fact specific developments of and methodologies for program budgeting. (Cost–benefit analysis, discussed peripherally in this article, to be addressed more fully in a future article introduces concepts of financial management into the budgeting process and because it is a form of alternatives analysis is related conceptually to program budgeting.)

A close reading of the literature reveals that enthusiasm for the latter two systems, both of which came to prominence in the last two decades, far outweighs actual experience with their implementation. A survey of large public libraries in 1977 revealed that 75 percent used the line-item format for budgeting (Prentice, 1977, 1983). Lynden's (1980) study of large university libraries indicated that most use some form of traditional, line-item budgeting; many combine this method with aspects of the newer methods. While the newer budgeting methods have rarely been fully implemented in libraries, they deserve attention to various aspects of institutional life, and they require analysis of processes and behavior. They encourage a fresh look at traditional library functions.

Line-Item or Incremental Budgeting

Almost all libraries maintain a chart of accounts for purposes of financial accounting. These records focus on the details of receipts and expenditures to support income statements, and upon changes in assets to develop balance sheets. Such accounts are almost always required to satisfy funding bodies that monies were spent as originally intended. Financial accounts of this type, usually cast in the line-item format, are used basically for *external* reporting.

When these line-item accounts are used as the basis for *internal* reporting and planning, they function as budgets. Traditionally, the individual categories of expense are reviewed, and increments are incorporated to meet anticipated increases in needs. This method focuses entirely upon "inputs".

The line-item budget is simple in the sense that it builds upon existing records. These records are by no means simple in themselves, and the method is not easy to implement. The complexity of line-item budgeting is well illustrated by a looseleaf notebook prepared for librarians in Ohio in 1969. The model is still useful since the line-item method of budgeting has not changed significantly in the intervening years (Clerk Treasurer, 1969). The manual includes legal documents, request forms, ledger sheets, a summary of library laws, and more. It gives instructions on how to keep financial records, prepare the budget document, and expenditures.

Another "how to" guide was prepared by Martin for academic libraries (1978). This work came out of much experience with budgets at the Pennsylvania State University Library. Martin guides the academic librarian through the steps necessary to gather data for the budget. He discusses methods of determining costs and formulating projections of future needs. Martin borrows some aspects of PPBS and ZBB in examining goals, but contends that the traditional emphasis upon categories of expenditure is the more realistic and practical method to adopt.

An eminently useable, and even charming, guide to line-item budgeting in the small public library can be found in Young's *The Library Trustee* (1978, pp. 161–167). Young suggests questions which might be asked in relation to the major line-item categories, and supplies a checklist for the budgeting process. This appendix, derived from work of the Library Development Bureau, New Jersey State Department of Education, raises questions which could be adapted for other types of libraries as well.

The principal dissatisfaction with line-item budgeting is that it tends to rigidify and ossify an organization. The argument takes the form that with a line-item budget, each year's budget tends to look just like last year's budget, just a little bit bigger. And last year's budget looks just like the budget of the year before, only just a bit bigger, etc. The pejorative term that has been coined for that effect is "disjointed incrementalism," i.e., each part continues to grow apace, regardless of whether the proportionality among parts remains appropriate. The thesis is that a line-item budget acquires inertia, and that each item continues to grow whether it should or not. Since a budget helps determine what an organization can do, the unfortunate effect is that the use of a line-item budget tends to impel an organization simply to do more of what it used to do, whether or not that still remains relevant. Peter Drucker is fond of pointing out that if there had been a U.S. Department of Labor at the turn of the century, there would still be programs in effect to aid displaced buggy whip manufacturers, regardless of the present relevance of such programs. The central theme of program budgeting and its off-springs, PPBS and ZBB, is that to budget and plan effectively, the organization must step back as it were, analyze its goals and objectives, and from that analysis determine what it will undertake and how it will deploy its resources—and it is from that step that the budget should be derived.

Formula Budgeting

During the past few years, interest has revived in a budgeting method which was developed during the 1960s. This method relates the "inputs" of users, academic programs, and bookstock to available funds. It is not, in contrast to program budgeting, a procedure by which to determine how resources are to be deployed, rather it is a mechanism by which a funding agency determines how to allocate funds among various functions serving a similar purpose.[1] In the case of libraries and information centers, the most typical example is that of a state distributing funds to various academic libraries. Whether there is any association between the formula budget as input determining mechanism, and how the library subsequently deploys its resources, the output process, is a function of the political context. In other words, the formula may have been based upon estimated costs for supporting students and faculty with adequate library resources in the physical sciences, social sciences, and humanities. That may or may not, however, constrain the library actually to purchase materials or expend its resources in those proportions.

Recent writing on this program budgeting method consists largely of exigeses of a document produced by the University of Washington. In 1968, a committee consisting of the business officers of several public institutions of higher learning in Washington State issued a document which described a method for allocating state funds to their institutions. They devised a formula for this apportionment which divided library functions into public service, technical services, and administration. The determination of appropriate levels of support for these functions was based upon the number of students in each unit, the level of degrees sought by these students, the size of the existing collection, and the rate of growth. While the document claimed to be a mathematical model for appropriating funds, it became the symbol of the formulaic approach (Model Budget Analysis System, 1968). This work was itself based upon previous studies. Clapp and Jordan (1965) had attempted to describe minimum standards for academic and research libraries. They provided the concept of weighing the students according to level of study in trying to assess their needs. Their formulas reflected current practice in established libraries.

The Washington State group looked carefully at attempts in the state of California to prescribe staffing levels at academic libraries according to formula. They acknowledged a debt also to the Massachusetts Institute of Technology (MIT).

The Washington State *Model* included some caveats which seem to have been ignored by many of those who transferred the technique to their own states or institutions. The authors, business managers all, noted that the state is necessarily involved in providing resources for academic libraries. If it is not given quantitative guidelines and recommendations by the institutions, it will make simplistic determinations of its own. For political reasons, it is wise to draw up guidelines for legislators based upon programs and objectives. Further, the authors warn that the level of support described in the formula is at a "threshold" level, not an optimum level. And finally, the authors might have added, but did not, that the formula approach had been worked out for allocating monies *among* institutions, but it had not been developed or tested for allocating monies *within* institutions.

The other classic work on formula budgeting is the study by Allen (1972). Allen undertook the study while on leave from the University of Washington. Comparing PPBS and Formula Budgeting, he concludes that the latter form, then in effect at his own institution, is clearly the preferable approach for allocating monies to institutions. This of course is not the same thing as the institution determining how to allocate the monies it has received. Allen (1972, p. 18) cites these virtues:

1. Formula budgeting is mechanical and therefore easier to prepare.
2. Because of its application to all institutions in the political jurisdiction for monies requested, political jockeying among institutions is substantially eliminated.

3. The governing bodies have a sense of equity because each institution in the system is measured against the same criteria.
4. Fewer budgeting and planning skills are required to prepare and administer a formula budget.

Allen examines the formulas of all the units he could identify that used such a procedure. They include the University of California, California State College, the State Universities of New York, Florida, Washington, and Texas, and the Canadian province of Ontario. In his main text, he evaluates these formulas and points to dangers in their execution. It is in his appendices, however, that his most interesting and oft-quoted observations appear. In a critique of the limitations of this approach, he notes that the formula designates *minimal* necessary funding; the governing unit may not understand this point. There is no authority to whom one can appeal should the integrity of the formula process break down. Nonformula items may seem to be luxuries. There is no provision for recovery from lean years. The formula encourages the proliferation of advanced degree programs. It does not account for cooperative ventures. It does not account for one-time-only costs. The list of limitations is long indeed, and the slightly exasperated tone of the presentation leads one to think that Allen's experience with this approach was fraught with frustration.

Allen sent a questionnaire to several large academic libraries to find out what forms of budgeting were used and which were anticipated. In his Appendix B he reveals that four libraries use line-item budgets, four use a formula of some sort, none use PPBS or zero-based forms, and a few use modifications and combinations. Of thirteen libraries responding to his question on direction, six reported that no change was expected. Some mild enthusiasm was expressed for PPBS. Allen noted that little creative energy seemed to go into budgeting (p. 8) and that a sense of helplessness seemed to prevail (p. 10).

During the last ten years, the notion of *formula budgeting* has cropped up sporadically. In 1975, Axford, who had championed the application of formula budgeting in the state of Florida, described its limitations in a rueful tone. He noted that the ideal formula he envisioned had been modified to meet political exigencies. The intent and the rationale of the formula had been all but lost in the appropriations process of the legislature.

In a particularly thoughtful and even-handed analysis, Summers (1975) examined the application of formula budgeting and drew conclusions about its usefulness to libraries. He pointed out the formulas were based upon standards of collection size and services, and that standards seemed to have had little effect on either libraries or on their governing bodies. The formulas were not, therefore, grounded in commonly accepted objectives. It was only, he noted, when accreditation was threatened that parent institutions seemed concerned with standards developed outside the institution.

Summers surmises that public higher education has been enthusiastic about formulae in part because the approach "connotes an air of mathematical infallibility" (p. 633). He points out that allocations are made primarily on a per capita basis, variously weighted, and that this unit is only a gross measure of library needs.

He echoes the Washington report in stating that formulae codify existing situations. Current inequities are perpetuated and one must resort to political activity to correct the situation. Summers observes that each president he consulted thought that the formula should be altered to favor his institution.

Summers concludes with the warning that the formula approach can lead to excessive emphasis upon productivity, an ill-defined concept in library service. While this approach may be useful for allocating resources, he contends that it cannot automatically "rationalize the allocation process and make it objective" (p. 636–37).

One must go back to the middle of the 1970s to find advocates of formula budgeting which is based upon per capita use modified by the size of the collection and rate of growth. Those who favored this form of budgeting typically argue that some quantification is necessary and formulas seem the obvious answer in that they are relatively simple to use. Reporting on the formula adopted for the State University of New York, Fairhold (1974) follows this pattern. He argues that the budget is an articulation of needs in a comprehensive format and that quantification is a way of providing legislators and librarians with a common language. He describes the creation of standard work units in state supported university and college libraries, and the creation of a model to quantify this activity. Enthusiastic as he is about formula budgeting, he notes that some flexibility is necessary and that one-time costs are difficult to justify in this system. Fairhold does not consider other methods of measuring library needs and activities which might meet the requirements of legislators and librarians.

Formula Budgeting, defined here as based upon per capita formulas, is still discussed in the literature. The more recent discussions of this approach tend to focus upon its applications to one particular aspect of library operations, that is, collection development.

An example of this genre is the report entitled *MIT Libraries, Collection Analysis Project* (MIT, 1978). While the Task Force mentions that the emphasis is upon subject, further discourse reveals that the ultimate determinant for the level of collecting in a subject is the number of students enrolled in that particular field or subject (p. 3). The project staff recommend that the library monitor expenditures closely through improved quantification techniques.

Schad (1978) traces the history of allocation formulas for collection development from the 1930s to the present. He restates the thesis of McGrath, Huntsinger, and Barbar that three factors are pertinent in constructing collection development formulas for the allocation of funds: enrollment, circulation, and citation patterns (p. 329). McGrath (1978, 1979, 1983) later examined numerous factors which affect the use of library materials and concluded that one could allocate along two lines with equal effectiveness. One could allocate according to the number of master's students in various fields, or one could apportion according to the degree to which a field had a recognized body of theory and literature.

Schad points out that McGrath assumes that use equals need, and that he ignores altogether unfilled demand (p. 329). Schad reminds formula enthusiasts that solutions which incorporate statistics simply perpetuate past patterns. Pointing out other methodological inconsistencies, Schad cautions that "a formula or model is only useful to the degree that it reflects accurately the realities of any situation and that more than a model can deliver should not be claimed" (p. 33). He concludes that the best general treatment of materials allocations is still the ALA "Guidelines for the Allocation of Library Materials Budgets."

While Schad's caveats are appropriate in a field where practitioners tend to get carried away by fadish approaches to managerial problems, his dismissal of McGrath's work is somewhat casual. Indeed, McGrath's work is making much the same point, that supposed subtlety in program budgeting in fact appears to produce very little if any increase in fit.

One could accept Schad's perceptive statement that "apportioning materials budgets is a collection development problem" and still use formulae, properly devised to guide the library in allotting funds to various fields and programs represented by its clientele. He assumes that collection builders thought that the formula could make the choices for them when he admonished that "there are no shortcuts" (p. 331). Schad exhibits a certain impatience with theory which characterizes many seasoned and beleaguered library directors.

Performance Budget

A performance budget is one in which the organization's budget is based upon the development of unit costs for the specific operations that the organization performs. For example, one might determine the performance items of a library to be items like: answering spot reference questions, undertaking online searches, preparing bibliographies, ordering and processing books, circulating books, etc. A unit cost can be developed for each of these items, that is, it cost x cents to circulate a book, y dollars and z cents to process a new book, etc. The budget of the library would then be the volume of the activities anticipated for the year multiplied by the unit cost of those activities at the appropriate level of volume.

Such a budget presentation superficially appears quite plausible—indeed, it appears scientific and quantitative. Koenig (1980), however, argues that it has two major drawbacks. First of all, the costing of activities is a very complex subject. Costs tend to behave in variegated fashions, and not to vary linearly. The cost of additional units of performance is not the full cost, but the marginal or incremental cost. Those marginal costs are apt to be substantially different from full unit costs (generally but not always lower) and this fact must be kept constantly in mind. Such ramifications are difficult to convey in a performance budget without the budget documentation and presentation becoming so elaborate that it sorely tries the patience of anyone reviewing it. Similarly, the interrelationship of costs of different operations is very complex. Different activities share certain "joint" costs. If one activity is cancelled or reduced, the unit cost for another may thereby increase. If these relationships are included in the budget presentation, it becomes even more cumbersome. But, if those relationships are not included, the result of a decision in regard to one portion of a budget may result in undertaking certain other activities at costs that are no longer realistic or attainable (this point surfaces again in discussions of ZBB, Zero Base Budgeting).

The second major problem with performance budgeting as Koenig analyzes it, is that it is too likely to simply be impolitic. A performance budget presentation seems to beg the reviewing authority to ask such questions as, "Why does it cost $1.43 to circulate a book? We can buy paperbacks cheaper than that." Library operations are often complex, and as Librarians from Panizzi to the present day have discovered, their complexity and even their very necessity are frequently difficult and time-consuming to explain to reviewing authorities.

A performance budget is to a degree somewhat more sophisticated than a line-item budget. It does allocate costs such as salaries and telephone charges to the different activities being performed—circulation, processing, reference, etc. However, it still does not explain to administration the purpose of the activities—who, for example, and what programs are being supported by on-line reference service? A performance budget looks convincingly quantitative but, in fact, almost invites a reviewing authority to take pot shots at it—to ask questions such as "Why are we doing this?" or "Is it necessary to do this or that in such an expensive fashion?"

The fact that performance budgets are very little used is perhaps the most convincing argument concerning their relative lack of advantage.

Program Budgeting

Program budgeting attempts to answer the basic questions of "to what purpose is the money being spent?, what programs are being supported? and what proportions of the institution's resources are being deployed to support each program?'' By contrast the basic function of a line-item budget is to answer the question ''on what items is the money being spent and to whom is the money being delivered?''

Indeed as Prentice (1983) points out, the focus of traditional line-item budgeting is accountability. For governmental and tax supported institutions, a line-item budget is generally a legal requirement, a requirement that typically derives from turn of the century anti-corruption in public office legislation. The line-item budget is therefore in a fundamental fashion related to external financial accounting and the stewardship of funds.

Program budgeting in a sense is not an alternative to a line-item budget, but an extension of it—an extension as it were of a one-dimensional list to a two-dimensional array, the second dimension comprising the allocations of the individual lines to the various programs. This is best illustrated by an example. In Figure 1 is a greatly simplified rendition of a program budget for an information center. The line-item budget is in fact embedded in, or is the basis of, the program budget. The left- and right-hand columns are in fact a line-item budget.

One of the rare treatments of program budgeting, as a technique in its own right, as distinct from the more elaborate versions, PPBS and ZBB is found in Koenig's *Budgeting Techniques for Libraries and Information Centers* (Koenig, 1980). Concerned with the politics of presentation, Koenig argues that the program budget is the most convincing form for a budget request. He prefers the program method because of its richness of detail and because of the ability it provides to link the performance of the unit with the goals and objectives of the parent organization.

Koenig also makes the point that the choice of what constitutes a program is entirely unstandardized, and is entirely a pragmatic local decision. Programs can be defined in many ways, particularly for a service function such as a library or information center. Programs can be defined in terms of services provided, departments serviced, organizational outputs supported, etc. The choice is ultimately a political one.

The program budget, according to Martin (1982), is particularly appropriate in a contracting economy. He sees program budgeting

Kostam Industries Incorporated
Information Services Department
Proposed Budget F.Y. 1986

Line Item	Budget Code	Data Supply	Current Awareness	Reference & Search	Issues Analysis	Prop. Data	Line Total
Compensation—Exempt	1101	36,000	12,500	22,700	38,000	24,000	133,200
Comp.—Non Exempt	1102	40,000	4,000	6,000	4,500	17,000	72,000
Books & Subscriptions	5011	110,000	—	3,000	3,000	1,000	117,000
D.P.—Internal	2001	3,000	3,500	—	—	46,000	52,500
D.P.—External	2002	—	17,000	70,000	20,000	4,000	111,000
Telecommunications	2101	—	2,000	3,000	1,800	1,000	7,800
Subcontracts	4101	—	6,000	4,000	15,000	—	25,000
Supplies	5001	8,500	1,500	1,200	1,200	3,400	15,800
Overhead	6000	32,000	6,000	4,000	3,500	12,000	57,000
Program Total		229,500	52,500	113,900	87,000	108,900	591,800 Grand Total

Figure 1. Program Budget (Simplified) in a Matrix Display.

91

as the most practical of the newer methods in that it requires relatively little staff time and paperwork. Martin advises that libraries find out what they are doing, then make value judgements about various activities, and finally make decisions about the allocations of resources. Martin's final words echo Koenig's contention that the program budget is the most effective and sophisticated method for explaining needs to funding bodies.

Planning–Programming Budgeting System

PPBS, an extension of program budgeting, achieved notoriety during the 1960s. It is associated with the U.S. Department of Defense under Ford "Whiz Kid" Robert McNamara during Lyndon B. Johnson's presidency. Libraries took note of this method during the early 1970s. In 1974 Gerald Shields observed that libraries, with their usual sense for ill-timing, were jumping on this bandwagon just as it was pulling out of town (Shields, 1974).

The basic elements of PPBS are these (Chen, 1980):

1. System concept and output orientation
2. Identifiable and measurable outputs
3. Stated objectives
4. Consideration of alternative means to achieve objectives
5. Activities grouped into program categories
6. Measured progress toward objectives
7. Analysis of benefits in relation to costs
8. Long-range planning

In summary, this method encourages the identification of goals and the measurement and evaluation of output. It thus focuses upon performance. It attempts to be objective and thus requires the quantification of output which is, in the case of the library, a service function. The representation of service in quantified terms presents particular difficulty to the adherents of this method. PPBS is not synonymous with program budgeting, as it is often described, for example by Drott (1978), but is a very specific implementation of program budgeting.

The recent literature on PPBS typically appears in the form

of prescriptive articles or papers. Empirical reportage is unusual since full implementation is rare. Treatises on PPBS, usually short, include many in the horatory mode. A few of the more recent works are critical and analytical (H. Young, 1976).

While many libraries are using elements of PPBS, little is now being written about the technique (Lynden, 1980; Prentice, 1977, 1983). In order to understand PPBS concepts which are being used in libraries, one must go back to writing from the early 1970s. The most frequently cited source of information of this budgeting technique as applied to libraries is a volume edited by Shields (1974), consisting of articles published during the early 1970s.

In his introduction, Shields noted that PPBS is tied to the concepts of accountability. Noting this connection Hannigan (1974, p. 71) warns that accountability should not require the sacrifice of principle for expedience. In a generally enthusiastic article, she recommends PPBS as a "sensible and satisfactory means to an end." She suggests that the goals be drawn in part from the recently published *Standards for School Media Programs*. Hannigan suggested ways in which media activities might be expressed in PPBS terms. This article reflects a confidence in standards and in PPBS which was pervasive in the early 1970s.

Howard (1974) also recommends PPBS claiming that it is suitable for the library manager wanting to become involved in community affairs, attempting to cope with change, or simply to quantify for improved efficiency (pp. 47–48). Howard admits that PPBS is somewhat baffling: "like an expensive fur coat on a cocktail waitress—beautiful to look at but hard to explain" (p. 56).

Howard, the director of the Vigo County Public Library, attempted to use this method. He informed and surveyed his community as a first step. He prepared forms for the gathering of data within the library. He admits that the beginnings were traumatic. The relationship of current output to achievement of objectives, he observes ruefully, was hard to determine (p. 58). The cost per output seemed high and the library was reluctant to publish these figures as part of the justification of the budget (p. 62). Despite drawbacks, Howard reports that the use of the technique led to the development of new services, including research for local government personnel, and new procedures were adopted which better suited the services of the library (pp. 59–61).

Even in Vigo County, which is often cited as the premier example of public library use of PPBS, the system was not implemented in its pure form. Howard notes that Indiana laws require line-item budgeting for reporting purposes (p. 62).

Schultz (1974) discusses the application of the technique to law libraries. He advocates PPBS with reservations. Schultz calls the method "Program Budgeting" but clearly describes a PPBS system with an emphasis upon outputs.

In PPBS's favor, Schultz points out that while the technique may be perceived as dehumanizing, it allows libraries to compete with other parts of the governmental unit who speak in the quantified language acceptable to budget allocators (p. 120). He warns, though, that statistical methods are expensive and difficult to use properly. He contends that it may be cheaper for the staff to use flow charts and to estimate expenses rather than undertake an extensive cost analysis. The exercise of tracking activities and costs, even if done informally, can lead to better procedures.

Schultz believes that the techniques should be applied only to those functions which are done repeatedly. He notes that one must develop a way of measuring work units and he mentions work by the ALA Statistical Coordinating Committee and the U.S. Bureau of the Budget. He concludes that the method should help librarians to show how much better service will be if a certain amount of additional money is allotted to the library (p. 129).

Schultz's article, like many on budgeting, has as its purpose the advocacy of a specific method. The article has little to say about how the method would be implemented. One cannot tell from the article whether the author has had practical experience with the method under discussion.

The reader has similar difficulty in assessing the practical nature of Fazar's advice in an article on measurement of activity and budgeting (1974). Fazar observed that the process of quantification was the knottiest issue in the use of PPBS. He contended that Operations Research would be helpful and he advocates the use of linear programming, queuing theory, gaming, mathematical modeling, and Program Evaluation and Review Techniques (critical path methodology). He sees quality control as the most difficult issue and cited efforts by the American Society for Quality Control to quantify quality. Again, there is no apparent evidence that the advice is based on operational experience.

Another significant document in the literature on PPBS was the publication of papers from a conference held at the Eastern Michigan University (Lee, 1973). While the work was issued prior to Shields' compilation, the papers generally postdate the contents of Shields. One has the peculiar sensation in reading this volume that one is hearing about sightings of a unicorn. None of the participants had experienced the application of PPBS to libraries. Philip Jager and Donald Lelong describe the use of the method in higher education. In Jager's case, it is once again difficult to know whether the proponent had actually experienced the implementation of PPBS (Jager, 1973). Lelong (1973) describes a modified version used by the state of Michigan.

A particularly useful contribution to this volume is the bibliography of some 490 items, on PPBS prepared by Eide (1973). Eide lists some 24 items dealing with the application of PPBS to libraries (p. 110). These date from 1966 to 1970 and consist mainly of systems approaches to library management. Among the periodical articles listed, most are very short, theoretical attempts to identify the usefulness of PPBS for libraries. The list of books and articles on the application of PPBS in government and education is considerably longer, and the aims more ambitious than the library literature.

In a lengthy treatise on PPBS, published in 1976, Harold Young observed that library literature lacks the critical commentary available on PPBS in other settings such as government and business (p. 15). He concentrates upon the difficulties and complexities of using an analytical system like PPBS where extensive quantification is necessary. He surmises that early experiments with modified PPBS methods were encouraging because of the Hawthorne Effect.

In Young's view, the successful use of PPBS requires a strong central authority. This condition may not exist in many contemporary institutions. Young further cautions that numerical data might be misinterpreted by outsiders and should be circulated selectively, advice similar to that of Koenig in regard to performance budgeting (Koenig, 1980). Young, nonetheless, recommends the use of PPBS. He concludes that it is the process, not the result, that makes the effort worthwhile. Drawing from J. L. Schofield, Young claims that the exercise of PPBS will force those concerned with library problems to face up to the real objectives of the institution, to understand the necessity for expenditures, to review existing programs, to consider alternatives, to insure target goals, and to review performance (p. 34). Young stresses the need for good data. In particular, he cites the need for an understanding of the client group. Young's perceptions on this point were shared by many library managers in the late seventies, and customer/community/user group surveys on the model created by Donald King have indeed proliferated (King, 1973).

Young reports the results of a questionnaire sent to 76 major university libraries on the subject of budget implementation. In 1971, half of these libraries were considering using some part of PPBS. In 1976, Young discovered that in fact none of these libraries had adopted PPBS in anything like its full form (p. 38).

In a recent article on the use of PPBS, Marilyn Sharrow describes a typical adaptation of the method. In order to accommodate a major budget reduction, the staff of the University of Toronto Library followed the steps of PPBS to analyze all expenditures, direct and indirect, and to relate them to appropriate applications in programs of activities. The institution chose the PPBS system, according to Sharrow, because quoting from Sturtz, it "represents a means of combining these traditional concepts of public budgeting into a package which allows systematic application of scientific techniques to total governmental planning, programming, and budgeting" (Sharrow, 1983, pp. 205–206).

In the manner of very recent budgeting articles, Sharrow dwells more upon process than upon format. The author fully acknowledges the problems encountered in moving through the steps of PPBS. She nonetheless advocates using this or similar budgeting methods. The figures, Sharrow maintains, "are extremely useful in determining future priorities and direction, in requesting funds, and in justifying the value of libraries and their services" (p. 207).

In its heyday, PPBS was much linked in the literature to MBO, management by objectives, both building upon the notion of defining goals, and defining quantifiable measures representing the attainment of those goals. It was frequently pointed out however that such quantification, often very difficult in any case, was particularly difficult in the case of public service organizations such as libraries. The enthusiasm for both systems, or at least the trendiness, has faded substantially, but as Koenig (1980) points out, there are three fundamental notions behind PPBS that remain intact:

> What is fundamental in the notion of PPBS is that budgeting should start with goals. The determination of dollar figures and organizational impact then follows.
>
> A second and somewhat subtler notion is that goals should be defined at as high an organizational level as possible in order to avoid "suboptimization."
>
> The third basic notion of PPBS is that of deciding upon measurable goal indicators that can be monitored and used to evaluate the attainment of goals.

Zero-Based Budgeting

In its emphasis upon outputs and quantification, zero-based budgeting (ZBB) has much in common with PPBS; it is of course another wrinkle upon program budgeting. ZBB includes one significant additional step, the necessity of justifying each part of the program every year. One assumes a budget of "zero" for each program until he/she can convince the appropriating body that the program is worthwhile and deserving of support at a specified level.

ZBB was developed in the early 1970s by Peter Phyrr (1970) at Texas Instruments for use in budgeting in a research and development (R&D) environment. The method was adopted by Jimmy Carter when he was governor of Georgia, and is alleged to have been one of the major mechanisms catapulting him to national attention. ZBB was applied to varying degrees in nonprofit institutions through the 1970s. One sees comparatively little about the method in the 1980s, though it is mentioned in passing as one budgeting tool among many. The method turned up in library literature in the late 1970s. Straightforward expositions of the method are set forth by Chen (1980) and Koenig (1980).

ZBB is a planning process which requires complete review and justification of the entire budget request. Old programs and new are scrutinized in three basic steps:

1. Identification of the decision units
2. Formulation of decision packages
3. Ranking, consolidation, and resource

The theoretical attractiveness to ZBB is that like PPBS or any developed program budget, it can be used for both planning and control.

Chen addresses herself to a sophisticated audience which is considering using ZBB in a complex organization. She answers the questions "why" and "how to" in relation to the implementation of ZBB. Chen includes sample forms useful in ZBB implementation. The numerous explanatory diagrams are ingenious, appropriate, and comprehensible. While the graphic work is not exemplary, the extent of the sample material is laudable.

Despite the rigor and sophistication of the presentation, one is left with the nagging feeling that this method is not significantly different from PPBS and that the same draw-backs applicable to PPBS also apply to ZBB. Outputs are difficult to measure in either design and the methodology employed in each does little to ameliorate this deficiency. In all fairness, one should admit that both PPBS and ZBB encourage a useful emphasis upon analysis and planning.

Koenig by contrast explains ZBB more briefly with the obvious assumption that a library is likely to undertake ZBB only in the context of the parent organization adopting ZBB, in which case he recommends that there be a formal program set up to train users in the intricacies of ZBB, and if no such program is planned, that one should "sit right down and write a memo to the highest figure in the corporate structure as is politic, and strongly recommend that there be one." Koenig warns of the complexities of the unavoidable interrelationships of decision packages such as joint costs across decision packages, and points out that the principal criticism of ZBB is that implementing such a program requires a great deal of effort and typically seems to result in very little change. He does point out one notion that he describes as potentially being very useful in more conventional and less cumbersome budget presentations. That notion is the one of presenting different programs (decision packages) at different levels of implementation. He argues that this which is in effect adding a third dimension to the conventional program budget presentation (see Figure 1) can contribute to the richness and depth of a budget presentation, and that such richness and depth contributes to the success of a presentation.

A basic weakness in the application of ZBB to libraries is that it is not particularly pertinent to the concept of the "going concern." Libraries, unlike research units of Texas Instruments, cannot start up or terminate service units without jeopardizing their basic mission. Serials, for example, are often more useful when they have been collected for many years. A broken run is difficult to control and to use. Is it meaningful to ask the serials librarian to justify all expenses on this type of material every year. If one were to start or discontinue story hours every year or so, would patrons remember to attend when they are offered? Is there not a necessity in libraries for offering a service over a long period and educating users in taking advantage of the service? Is is wise to disrupt the habits of library users? Is ZBB realistic in an educational or service institution where the patron would have difficulty responding to periodic change? Assuredly one needs to look at alternatives, but in an ongoing service context ZBB may be a far more powerful and disruptive tool than is needed to accomplish that objective. The notion of different levels of implementation for specific decision packages addresses this concern to a degree, but only to a degree.

If any writing on budgeting can be described as compelling, it is the account of the person who has tried the technique under discussion. Even in a short and tightly constructed presentation, through the medium of microform, one can detect traces of emotion. Diane Parker and Eric Carpenter issued a report of this nature, in this format, in 1979. They described the use of ZBB in the Lockwood Library, State University of New York at Buffalo (Parker and Carpenter, 1979). The technique was used to justify staffing requests. This method was chosen because it eliminated historical justifications and forced an objective and detailed examination of functions. Parker and Carpenter report that the library emphasized two aspects of ZBB: the development of decision packages and the ranking of them. While judging the experiment to be a success, the authors admit—and here one hears a sigh—that it is difficult to include all aspects of an operation in the analysis. They do agree that the process forced the library to re-examine some basic assumptions.

Another first-hand account is provided by Arthur Gesch of Milwaukee Public Library (Gesch, 1979). Gesch's description of the first phases of this undertaking provides insight into the politics of implementation. The library sent staff to a seminar at

Marquette University to learn about the technique. Volunteers were then sought who would be willing to try out the techniques in their units. The volunteers then attended a training program sponsored by the city. Each participant then did an analysis of his/her unit on ZBB principles. They met, coordinated these results, and tackled the overall budget.

Gesch reports these benefits: the library was ready for the mayor's efforts to apply ZBB city-wide; the participating librarians improved their skills; and an improved analysis of costs resulted. The need for better control was apparent to all.

Like other institutions, Milwaukee Public Library discovered that ZBB is time and paper consuming. ZBB must be tailored to fit the individual institution. On the plus side, participants become more aware of the budget. Some services, Gesch contends, are necessary for minimal operation, such as heat and light, and are therefore not subject to questioning along ZBB lines. Finally, libraries do not have the data necessary for detailed cost analysis. Implicit in Gesch's account is the assumption that the library had to attempt ZBB in order to meet the mayor's demands for accountablity in city agencies. It seems probable that the library would not have undertaken this form of self study if this incentive had not been present.

Since implementation of ZBB is relatively rare, sample forms are hard to come by. Sample materials from the University of Toronto can be found in the "Spec Kit" entitled *Cost Studies and Fiscal Planning* (ARL, 1977a).

Other sample material, prepared for a fictitious library, can be found in Benjamin Speller's *Zero-Base Budgeting for Libraries* (1979). This publication, produced for a workshop on ZBB, includes an essay by Charles Sargent which treats the concept of marginal utility embodied in ZBB. While the material in this work is somewhat superficial, it is useful as an introduction to the steps in implementing ZBB. The authors deemphasize the mathematical complexities of calculating costs and stress the conceptual aspects of the method. The workbook concludes with a description of a computer application package to support ZBB.

In an article from the previous year, Speller warned that computer applications cannot be relied upon to supply the "right" decision package. It can only provide supporting data. The manager must still make the crucial decisions (Speller, 1978).

In selecting one or another of these budgeting methods, the library manager would do well to keep in mind the recommendation of the faculty committee of the library, Rutgers University: "It is our general recommendation that the library Administration not be preoccupied with methodology such as formula vs. program budgeting as long as key budget functions are being performed, there is participation in the budgeting process, and the budget supports the goals of the Library" (ARL, 1977b).

Program Analysis

Program budgeting is very much related to the concept of program analysis. The fundamental idea behind program or programmatic analysis is that of looking at an operation of organization in terms of what its outputs or programs are, and what inputs and resources are deployed to support those outputs. In short, program analysis is the analysis of an operation or an organization in terms of what its goals and objectives are. The examination of resource deployment means of course that program analysis is also a budgeting analysis.

The classic example of program analysis in library and information systems remains Raffel and Shishko's study of the MIT library system in 1969 (Raffel and Shishko, 1969). The results of that study contain a number of useful insights. For example, the MIT library system spends more money housing readers than it does housing books, and that is probably not atypical. Another insight is that when analyzed in terms of its programs, supporting undergraduate education versus supporting research, for example, an academic "research library" such as MIT has a smaller research component than many "special libraries" in industrial research settings. Perhaps the most useful insight in the study was the extent of the tradeoffs and the possible alternatives between library study space, dormitory study space, and various document delivery mechanisms.

Such programmatic analysis is indeed the foundation of much long range planning; and conceptually at least is the foundation of much of the development of library planning procedures in the 1970s such as the MRAP program (Webster, 1974). These developments have been discussed in a previous article in this journal (Koenig and Kerson, 1983).

THE TREATMENT OF BUDGETING IN LIBRARY MANAGEMENT TEXTBOOKS

A comparison of the new edition of Wheeler and Goldhor's *Practical Administration of Public Libraries* (1981) with Rogers and Weber's *University Library Administration* (1971) illustrates the changes in approach to budgeting which have taken place over the decade. These texts represent the assimilation of budgeting theory into library practice. Rogers and Weber, a decade ago, defined the budget as a"formalized statement of all accounts having monies available for a specified period. . .allocated according to categories (books, binding, equipment, travel) or operating units (Catalog Department, Chemistry Library, Administrative Department)" (p. 89). They thus describe a line-item, object-of-expenditure, or traditional budget. The terms are used interchangeably.

Rogers and Weber note that "no university library should operate without a set of goals." They indicate thereby an awareness of concerns which came to the fore with PPB and ZBB. The authors speak of grouping expenditure: maintenance, improvement, and capital funds—thus raising other issues associated with program budgeting and PPB. They speak in an informal way of priorities, standards, and formulas.

Rogers and Weber advocate the use of performance analysis and program planning based upon identified objectives and on objective analyses of cost. They note that although the director may not be asked to present his/her entire budget in this form, he/she may be asked to justify significant changes in this manner. Where conventional budgeting is used, they advise that a mere summary along PPBS lines may be adequate for justification. Lynden (1980) in a review of budgeting in academic libraries indicates that most large university libraries use traditional modes of budgeting.

Rogers and Weber warn that the creation of a budget takes a good part of the year and that the negotiations with the parent agency may take half a year. They further note that expenditures must be monitored periodically. The process is time consuming. It requires considerable delegation and staff involvement.

Carleton Rochell, who revised Wheeler and Goldhor (1981),

describes the budgeting process in a manner quite similar to Rogers and Weber. His work shows a greater concern for the political process. This interest may reflect both the current economic difficulties of libraries, indeed of the nation, and the nature of his audience, that is, public library administrators. Rochell is an academic librarian who spent many years in public libraries.

Rochell begins with observations on the function of the budget and its relationship to local government expenditures. He implies a concern about the source of funding and advocates involvement in the political process to insure adequate funding. Rochell's omissions are as significant as his inclusions. He does not claim, as do many advocates of the new quantified, planning systems, that the presentation of objectives in quantified form will help one to secure adequate funding. Nor, like Koenig, does he encourage the use of formulas or the citing of standards to convince funding agencies.

Rochell sees the rationale for budget requests flowing from local conditions. This statement is an implicit rejection of the formula or standards approach. He refers to the justification process of ZBB as appropriate.

Rochell, like Rogers and Weber, dwells on the time-table. He stresses the need to involve staff and to educate trustees and local officials.

While he mentions a variety of budget methods, such as ZBB and PPBS, he observes that most libraries use line-item or incremental budgeting for fiscal control and use some modification, usually a program budgeting approach such as a simplification of PPBS, for planning. He observes that it is not easy to mix the two.

Revealing both his awareness of theory, and his skepticism about it, Rochell concludes that while a great deal has been written, especially in recent years, about budgeting for public bodies, there is no one system that the enterprising library director can take off the shelf and apply without extensive study and perhaps modification and alteration to meet local conditions (p. 128).

Evans, in his *Management Techniques for Librarians* (1976; 2nd ed., 1983), admirably makes the point that the planning process and the budgeting process are inextricably linked. The primary emphasis of his book is upon line-item budgeting. In the first edition, 1976, performance budgeting and PPBS are discussed as well. The latter however is described as a variation of performance budgeting. The very real distinctions between performance budgeting and program budgeting is entirely missed. The second edition, 1983, fails to correct this very important error, though it does add some discussion of ZBB. Because of this confusion, the authors do not recommend Evans' chapter on Financial Control, though much of the remainder of the book is first rate.

Rizzo, in his *Management for Librarians* (1980) does not address budgeting per se, but does discuss it in passing, particularly in the context of planning. One very useful section however (Rizzo, pp. 287–288) is a discussion of the particular problems of budgeting for training and development. Like Koenig (1980), Rizzo points out the particular vulnerability of such funds, but pursues the topic in greater depth.

Steuart and Eastlick, in their 1977 textbook, *Library Management,* do little more than list the major budgeting techniques, not however including ZBB. Program budgeting is described as a "relatively new technique," and the link between PPBS and program budgeting is not recognized.

In summary, most of the library management textbooks assume a basic line-item approach with some discussion of, but little advocacy for, more sophisticated approaches.

BUDGET PRESENTATION

Drucker observed that libraries are budget-based (Drucker, 1976). By this, he meant that libraries derive their funds from governing bodies in response to their requests for given amounts. Libraries explain their needs to these parent units by means of their budgets or plans for expenditures. The document itself must be persuasive in order that the funds might be granted. While much advice is available on the use of various budgeting techniques, relatively little guidance can be found in the literature on the creation of the budget as physical document. And even less attention is given to the process of presenting the document and communicating with the governing unit.

One commentator who does focus upon budget presentation is Koenig (1977, 1980) who sees budgeting as a central determinant in shaping a library or information center and the nature of its operations. He believes that the attention given to the preparation of the budget is a "function of how innovative you plan to be in carrying out your responsiblity as a librarian" (Koenig, 1980, p. 1). The point is repeatedly made that the budgeting process is at least as much a political process as it is a quantitive financial process. Managers are advised to "take an accountant to lunch" and "to check the political wind," indeed there is a full chapter devoted to "Budgeting and Financial Politics." The librarian is further advised to choose a budgeting method which can be effectively communicated to the governing agency, and Koenig's preference is clearly for a program budget approach, but something less than PPBS or ZBB in complexity. He further suggests that some attention should be given to graphics used in the presentation.

White notes that librarians are not confrontive managers (1979). Acknowledging that confrontation may lead to dismissal, he nonetheless criticizes librarians for accepting budget cuts passively. He takes librarians to task for failing to dramatize their case "by pointing out what administrative action is doing to library programs, and to force the faculty to face the reality of what appears to be an enormous change in the value system for library acquisition. . . . Instead, librarians have taken on their shoulders the responsibility of trying to make materials budget curtailments make as little an impact as possible. . .[I]n being 'good soldiers,' they have certainly not gained faculty appreciation for their heroic efforts." It is by means of an effective budget presentation that library managers can make their plights known. White, like Koenig, counsels aggression in seeking funds.

Hennessy et al. (1976) look upon the budget document from the point of view of the governing unit. They mention the need to respond to recent demands for accountability, efficiency, and rationality. More specifically, they remind the preparers of library budgets that parent bodies think in terms of two categories of expenditures: revenue or annual expenses, and capital outlay. Libraries must present their budgets and plans so that the funding agencies can incorporate this information into their overall budget plan. The authors caution that a library is a not-for-profit enterprise and should not try to quantify all of its services as a business might. Further, the human factor must be kept in mind. Specific budgeting methods, like PPBS, should be considered only aids to help explain the library to the funding boards.

Prentice too considers the habits of the governing boards when she advises budget officers to become fully familiar with the economic base and condition of the community. The budget must be presented in a manner consistent with the historical pattern of budgeting in the community. Citing Wildavsky (1964), Prentice suggests that new ideas be repeated over a number of years in the budget so that the governing boards will get used to them (Prentice, 1977, p. 95). Taking a pragmatic approach, Prentice (p. 92) notes that the budget is a legal document or contract as well as a planning device. Prentice further advises that the library seek funds actively in concert with the policies of its governing board. The librarian should investigate the history and prospects of government funding through federal and state programs, local fund-raising possibilities, and bond issues. In addition to presenting a list of its needs, Prentice in the public arena, like Koenig in the corporate arena, advises the librarian to pursue ways of getting library funds from sources other than the immediate governing body.

Focusing on the physical document, Gelfand suggests that illustrations be used to improve the appearance of the work and to point up programs and activities of the library. He insists that the publicly issued budget must be clear and readable. He suggests, for the public library, that press releases be prepared to make the budget known to the community (Gelfand, 1972, p. 44). His suggestion is consistent with Koenig's concern for the appearance of the budget. Koenig found it useful to maintain a file of documents, clippings, etc., which could accompany or be used in support of the budget documents at the time of submission (Koenig, 1980, p. 49–52).

Commenting on style, Lynden reports that academic library directors have found brevity a virtue in the presentation of the document. They advocate including some text to explain new or extraordinary expenditures (Lynden, 1980, p. 103). Lynden believes that budgets should be explained in a low-key, calm tone. Documentation, such as newspaper articles, can be effective. Lynden reports that library directors consider an atmosphere of mutual trust essential to successful budget presentation. It is usual for the library director and the parent body to negotiate the figures long before the formal submission is made.

Lynden's remarks reiterate that the presentation of the budget is a political act. Koenig and White advise the librarian to accept this fact and to enter the political arena aggressively. Prentice cautions the librarian to be sensitive to political protocol and to become well informed about the economic and political realities of the community. Gelfand and Lynden provide some tips on making the budget document attractive, comprehensible and acceptable. Each of these suggestions seems to be rooted in experience with the presentations of budgets. These particular observations have been included in this survey because the authors consider them valid suggestions for improving the prospects for the acceptance of any type of budget for any type of library. They indeed constitute what the authors hope emerges as the central theme of this review, that while budgeting technique is indeed important, what is of central importance is the political context and the pertinence of technique to context.

NOTE

1. From the funding agencies point of view, a formula budget may of course be an output mechanism, but even here, the formula is apt more often to determine the proportional size of the pie to be allotted to each institution, not the absolute size of either the pie or the slice. From the recipients' point of view, it is an input mechanism.

REFERENCES

Association of Research Libraries, Systems and Procedures Exchange Center. *Cost Studies and Fiscal Planning.* Washington, D.C.: ARL, Office of University Library Management Studies, 1977. (a)

———*Preparation and Presentation of the Library Budget.* Washington, D.C. ARL, Office of University Library Management Studies, 1977. (b)

Allen, Kenneth. *Current and Emerging Budgeting Techniques in Academic Libraries Including a Critique of the Model Budget Analysis Program of the State of Washington.* Seattle, University of Washington, 1972.

Axford, H. W. "Effective Resource Allocation in Library Management," *Library Trends,* 23 (1975):551–572.

Chen, Ching-chih. *Zero-Base Budgeting in Library Management.* New York: Oryx Press, 1980.

Clapp, Verner W. and Robert T. Jordan. "Quantitative Criteria for Adequacy of Academic Library Collections," *College and Research Libraries,* 26 (September 1965):371–380.

Clerk Treasurer. *Clerk Treasurer's Handbook for Ohio Public Libraries.* Frances A. Krieger, comp. Columbus: Ohio Library Foundation, 1969.

Drott, E. Carl. "Budgeting for School Media Centers," *Drexel Library Quarterly,* 14, no. 3 (July 1978):78–93.

Drucker, Peter F. *Management, Tasks, Responsibilities, Practices.* New York: Harper & Row, 1974.

———"Managing the Public Service Institution," *College and Research Libraries,* 37, no. 1 (January 1976):4–14.

Evans, G. Edward. *Management Techniques for Librarians.* New York: Academic Press, 1976.

———*Management Techniques for Librarians, 2nd Edition.* New York: Academic Press, 1983.

Eide, Margaret. "PPBS: A Bibliographic Survey." In Sul H. Lee (ed.), *Planning-Programming-Budgeting System (PPBS): Implications for Library Management.* Ann Arbor: Plierian, 1973.

Fairhold, Gilbert W. "Essentials of Library Manpower Budgeting." In Gerald R. Shields and J. Gordon Burke (eds.), *Budgeting for Accountability in Libraries.* Metuchen, N.J.: Scarecrow, 1974, p. 81–96.

Fazar, Willard. "Program, Planning and Budgeting Theory: Improved Library Effectiveness by Use of the Planning-Programming-Budgeting System." in Gerald R. Shields and J. Gordon Burke. *Budgeting for Accountability in Libraries.* Metuchen, N.J.: Scarecrow, 1974, p. 96–118.

Gelfand, Morris Arthur. "Budget Preparation and Presentation: Creating a Favorable Climate for Budget Approval." *American Libraries,* 3 (May 1972):496–500.

Gesch, A. P. "ABB—Dry Run at MPL (Milwaukee Public Library)." *Wisconsin Library Bulletin,* 75 (1979):269–70.

Hannigan, Jane Anne. "PPBS and the School Media Center." In Gerald R. Shields and J. Gordon Burke (eds.), *Budgeting for Accountability in Libraries.* Metuchen, N.J.: Scarecrow, 1974, p. 71–80.

Hennessy, James, A., Beck, Terence, and Dixon, Angela. *Finance and Libraries.* Studies in Library Management, vol. 3. Hamden, Conn.: Linnet Books, 1976.

Horngren, Charles T. *Cost Accounting, A Managerial Emphasis.* Englewood Cliffs, N.J.: Prentice-Hall, 1972.

Howard, Edward N. "Toward PPBS in the Public Library." In Gerald R. Shields and J. Gordon Burke (eds.), *Budgeting for Accountability in Libraries.* Metuchen, N.J.: Scarecrow, 1974.

Jager, Philip. "The State of Michigan Program Budget Evaluation System as Applied to Higher Education." In Sul H. Lee (ed.), *Planning-Programming-Budgeting System: Implications for Library Management.* Ann Arbor: Pierian Press, 1973, p. 49–66.

King, Donald W. & Palmour, Vernon E. "User Behaviour." In *National Information Retrieval Colloquium Proceedings,* 1973, pp. 7–33. Washington, ASIS, 1973.

Koenig, Michael E. D. "Budgets and Budgeting." *Special Libraries,* 68 (1977):228–34, 235–40.

———*Budgeting Techniques for Libraries and Information Centers.* New York, N.Y.: Special Library Asso., 1980.

———"Fiber Optics and Library Technology." *Library Hi-Tech* 2(1) 1984:9–16.

Koenig, Michael E. D. and Kerson, Leonard. "Strategic and Long Range Planning in Libraries and Information Centers." In *Advances in Library Administration and Organization,* Vol. 2 (1983):199–258.

Lee, Sul H. *Planning-Programming-Budgeting System: Implications for Library Management.* Ann Arbor: Pierian Press, 1973.

Lelong, Donald C. "Planning, Programming, Budgeting Systems in Higher Education." In Sul H. Lee (ed.), *Planning-Programming-Budgeting System.* Ann Arbor: Pierian Press, 1973.

Lynden, Frederick C. "Library Materials Budgeting in the Private University Library: Austerity and Action." *Advances in Librarianship,* 10 (1980):89–154.

McGrath, William E. "Relationships Between Hard/Soft, Pure/Applied, Life/Non-Life Disciplines and Subject Book Use in a University Library." *Information Processing and Management,* 14 (1) 1978:17–28.

———"Two Models for Predicting Subject Circulation: A Contribution to the Allocation Program." *Journal of the American Society for Information Science* 30 (5) Sept. 1979:264–268.

———"Multidimensional Mapping of Book Circulation in a University Library." *College Research Libraries* 44 (2) (March 1983):103–115.

M.I.T. Libraries, Collection Analysis Project. Task force on budget allocation. (Cambridge, Ma.: M.I.T. Libraries), 1978.

Martin, Murray S. *Budgetary Control in Academic Libraries.* Greenwich, Conn.: JAI PRESS, 1978.

———"Budgeting—the practical way." *Canadian Library Journal,* 39 (1982):299–302.

Model Budget Analysis System for Program 05 Libraries. Prepared by the Interinstitutional Committee of Business Officers. (Washington): 1968.

Parker, D. C., and Carpenter, E. J. "Zero-base budget approach to staff justification for a combined reference and collection development department," in American Library Asso., Assoc. of College and Research Libraries. *New Horizons for Academic Libraries.* New York: Saur, 1979, p. 472–82.

Phyrr, Peter A. *"Zero-Base Budgeting." Harvard Business Review* 48 (6)Nov./Dec. 1970:111–121.

Prentice, Ann. *Public Library Finance.* Chicago, American Library Asso., 1977.

———"Strategies for Survival: Library Financial Management Today." *Library Journal,* Special report 7 (1978).

———*Financial Planning for Libraries.* Library Administration Series: 8. Metuchen, N.J.: Scarecrow, 1983.

Raffel, Jeffrey A. and Shishko, Robert. *Systematic Analysis of University Libraries: An Application of Cost-Benefit Analysis,* Cambridge, Mass., M.I.T. Press, 1969.

Management for Librarians: Fundamentals and Issues, Westport, Conn.: Greenwood Press, 1980.

Rogers, Rutherford D., and Weber, David. *University Library Administration.* New York: Wilson, 1971.

Schad, Jasper G. "Allocating Materials Budgets in Institutions of Higher Education." *Journal of Academic Librarianship,* (1978):328–332.

Schultz, Jon. "Program budgeting and work measurement for law libraries," in Gerald R. Shields, and J. Gordon Burke. *Budgeting for Accountability in Libraries.* Metuchen, N.J.: Scarecrow, 1974, p. 119–40.

Sharrow, Marilyn J. "Budgeting Experience—at the University of Toronto Library." *Canadian Library Journal,* 40 (1980):205–207.

Shields, Gerald R. and Burke, J. Gordon. *Budgeting for Accountability in Libraries.* Metuchen, N.J.: Scarecrow, 1974.

Smith, G. Stevenson. *Accounting for Librarians: and Other Not-for-profit Managers.* Chicago, American Library Association, 1983.

"Computer Applications for Zero Base Budgeting: Statement to Workshop Participants." *Library Acquisitions,* 2 no. 1 (1978):15–16.

Speller, Benjamin F., Jr. *Zero-based Budgeting for Libraries and Information Centers: A Continuing Education Manual.* Fayetteville, Ark.: Hi Willow Research and Publishing, 1979.

Steuart, Robert D. and Eastlick, John T. *Library Management.* Littleton, Colorado, Libraries Unlimited, 1977.

Summers, F. William. "The Use of Formulae in Resource Allocation." Library Trends, 23 (1975):631–42.

Webster, Duane E. "The Management Review and Analysis Program: An Assisted Self Study to Secure Constructive Change in the Management of Research Libraries." *College and Research Libraries,* 35 (2) (1974):114–125.

Wheeler, Joseph Lewis and Goldhor, Herbert. [Practical Administration of Public Libraries] rev. by Carlton Rochell, N.Y. Harper & Row, 1981.

White, Herbert S. "Budgeting Priorities in the Administration of Large Academic Libraries." In American Library Association, Association of College and Research Libraries. *New Horizons for Academic Libraries,* Saur Verlag, 1979.

———*Managing the Special Library.* White Plains, N.Y., Knowledge Industry Publications Inc., 1984.

Wildavsky, Aaron. *The Politics of the Budgetary Process.* N.Y.: Little, 1964.

Young, Harold Chester. *Planning, Programming, Budgeting Systems in Academic Libraries.* Detroit: Gale, 1976.

Young, Virginia G. *The Library Trustee, a Practical Guidebook.* New York and London: R. R. Bowker, 1978.

LIBRARY SUPPORT OF FACULTY RESEARCH:

AN INVESTIGATION AT A MULTICAMPUS UNIVERSITY

Barbara J. Smith

ABSTRACT

An examination of several aspects of library support of faculty research at a large multicampus university was undertaken over a two-year period. Discussions of whether library holdings support research, whether faculty see the library as helpful, and where faculty obtain research materials when the library fails them are presented.

Among the conclusions are the following: (1) faculty research is being supported rather well; (2) inadequate resources do not limit research; and (3) personal collections of materials are valuable to researchers.

Advances in Library Administration and Organization, Volume 4, pages 111–120.

INTRODUCTION

The Pennsylvania State University includes a central campus and twenty other campuses (only nineteen locations were included in the study) dispersed throughout the Commonwealth. The main campus contains the collections designated to support faculty research at all locations. The dispersed campus libraries support the teaching and service functions of those locations. Faculty at all locations, however, as mandated by University-wide promotion and tenure criteria are expected to conduct research and to engage in scholarly pursuits.

Given the fact that The Pennsylvania State University Libraries have a rather modest collection (2,402,938 cataloged volumes) among research libraries,[1] we have at times questioned our ability to serve our faculty at all our locations—hence, this study.

It was designed to determine if the University Libraries were able to adequately and equitably support faculty research at all locations where "adequately" was defined as having available for use a majority of the resources used in publication and "equitably," as showing no evidence of significant diffferences between use by main campus and branch campus faculty. An assumption was made that branch campus faculty knew and were willing to use the established procedures to provide access to the collections of the Libraries. The study was also designed to determine faculty perceptions of the usefulness of the Libraries in their research, e.g., did they give up or modify a research project because of limited library resources.

The study was conducted in two parts. Part one was conducted at the branch campuses and the results were published recently.[2] The second part was conducted in 1983 at the main campus. Summary data of the two parts of the study as well as comparative data are discussed here and form the basis for the conclusions drawn.

METHODOLOGY

Two methods of data collection were used, questionnaire and citation analysis. The questionnaire asked in general: a) what faculty preferences were as sources of material for their research and why they preferred those sources, and b) what they estimated to be the percentage of research resources they consulted that came from the University Libraries collections. The citation analysis[3] consisted of examining the references cited in articles (books were not included for several reasons, including the fact that it was felt that the number of references in book-length works would require more time and manpower available) published by faculty and comparing them to the resources available in the University Libraries which could have been consulted had the faculty chosen to use the Libraries' collections.

A sample (254 from a population of 2540) was drawn from those faculty who published articles in a two-year period. The resulting 298 articles and 3,672 citations were analyzed. The faculty who published the articles were mailed questionnaires and were asked to return them within a four-week period; 226 were returned, a response rate of 89 percent.

Tabulations of the questionnaire responses and citation analyses were made and appropriate statistical procedures were applied.

RESULTS

Citation Analysis

Eighty-six percent of all references cited in faculty publications in this study are available in the Libraries. For faculty publishing in the sciences 89 percent of the resources are available; 84 percent for the social sciences, and 73 percent for the humanities (see Table 1).

There were no significant differences between the number of references cited and the number of references available in the University Libraries for those faculty publishing at main campus and those publishing at the branch campuses. Needless to say, there should not have been since the faculty at all locations are accessing the same collections, but, for political reasons, this needed to be verified. Some concern has been expressed, also, that branch campus faculty publications would have fewer references and, at least in this study, such is not the case.

Table 1. Percentages of Cited References Available in Libraries

Subject Areas	All Locations N = 222	Branch Campuses N = 82	Main Campus N = 140
Sciences	89	88	89
Social Sciences	84	79	86
Humanities	73	70	88
Total	86	82	88

Questionnaire

Faculty were asked what they estimated was the percentage of materials used in their research that was obtained from the University Libraries. The faculty at the branch campuses estimated 54 percent, the main campus, 45 percent. Overall 48 percent of the material used in faculty research was estimated to have been obtained from the University Libraries.

When asked to rank the sources or methods used to obtain research materials, all faculty ranked their personal collections as the most frequent source. There was a significant difference between the ratings of the branch campus and main campus faculty, however. As might be expected, borrowing from the Penn State Libraries was the faculty's second choice. It is interesting to note that as their third choice branch campus faculty visit other libraries, main campus faculty visit the main campus library (see Table 2).

When asked why they rely on Penn State Libraries as a source of research material, both main campus and branch campus faculty indicated they used the Libraries because they have what they need. The second reason indicated for using the Libraries was that they felt it was an effective and efficient method of obtaining books and journal articles. It is interesting to note that when asked whether they structure their research to conform with the materials available in the Libraries, only 2 percent indicated they did. There were no significant differences between branch campus and main campus faculty ratings in this area (see Table 3).

The faculty at the main campus indicated that when they use the libraries at other institutions they do so because those libraries have the material needed. The branch campus faculty indicated

Table 2. Comparison of Mean Ratings (by Faculty) of Sources and
Methods of Obtaining Material

Methods or Sources of Material	Branch Campus N	$\overline{X}$	Main Campus N	$\overline{X}$	t-value
Personal collection	82	2.3	141	1.6	3.94*
Borrow from Penn State (intercampus loan)	81	2.4	132	2.3	.778
Use interlibrary loan	71	4.0	125	4.3	1.67
Borrow directly from Penn State Libraries	68	4.2	109	4.8	2.73*
Visit and work in Penn State Libraries	74	3.9	123	2.9	5.00*
Visit and work in non- Penn State Libraries	75	3.8	105	5.1	5.20*

Note: 1 = most frequent; 6 = least frequent. T–test applied. Intercampus Loan refers to loan of materials among Penn State Libraries.
*Significant at the .05 level.

that they used other libraries because other libraries were more convenient. It was expected that branch campus faculty would find "methods too inefficient" and "other libraries more convenient" reasons for using other libraries more than main campus faculty; these differences are significant (see Table 4). (At least six of the Penn State branch campuses are within easy driving distance of the bibliographic riches of Philadelphia and Washington; four can easily reach New York City; and five are an hour or two from Pittsburgh.)

Table 3. Comparison of Mean Ratings (by Faculty) of Reasons for Using
University Libraries

Factors	Branch Campuses N	$\overline{X}$	Main Campus N	$\overline{X}$	t-value
Have materials needed	35	1.1	57	1.1	.44
Effective and efficient methods	33	1.5	57	1.7	1.00
Other libraries not convenient	34	1.8	57	2.0	.833
Structure research based on collection	33	2.9	57	2.7	1.33

Note: 1 = most frequent; 6 = least frequent. T–test applied.
No significance shown at the .05 level.

Table 4.   Comparison of Mean Ratings (by Faculty) of Reasons for *Not*
Using the University Libraries

Factors	Branch N	Campuses $\overline{X}$	Main N	Campus $\overline{X}$	t-value
Not aware of holdings	47	2.7	86	2.7	.44
Do not have needed materials	47	2.3	86	2.1	1.33
Methods too in- efficient	48	2.0	86	2.6	3.31*
Other libraries more convenient	46	1.6	86	2.7	8.31*

Note: 1 = most frequent; 6 = least frequent. T–test applied.
 *Significance at the .05 level.

N.B.   The data displayed in Tables 3 and 4 are the results of two parts of
one question on the questionnaire where faculty were asked to respond in such
a way that the N for that question is a total of the N's from both tables. (See
the Appendix, question 3.)

It was reassuring to find that only a small percentage of the
faculty replied that they had modified or given up a research
project because the University Libraries did not have the resources needed. Only nineteen percent of the branch campus
faculty and 14 percent of the main campus faculty responded
positively to this question. This is 16 percent overall.

COMMENTS

Of some 70 written comments received with the questionnaires,
few were negative. Hours were mentioned as too few. Several
negative comments were serious and attempts will be made to
deal with a good portion of them (e.g., unsatisfactory copy machines). Some were rather interesting: "I owe the library money
and rather than 'face the music' I tend to rely on my own materials." A library-to-faculty-office delivery service was mentioned (twice) as desirable.

CONCLUSIONS

From this study, it is reasonable to conclude that if faculty want to rely on the University Libraries, most (86 percent) of what they need for their publications is available. Although not a large research library, the collections at Penn State have apparently been chosen with the faculty's research needs in mind, especially in the sciences which represent the University's research strengths.

Since it has been shown that faculty rely on their personal collections for approximately half of their research needs, perhaps the Libraries staff should be working to a greater degree with faculty to identify more fully the materials faculty do not tend to keep in their own collections but need for research. Working with the graduate assistants who appear, from the comments submitted, to be the gatekeepers between the Libraries and the faculty to refine faculty needs is also desirable.

The branch campus faculty are apparently a resourceful lot. They, as well as the main campus faculty, seldom "give up" due to lack of library support even though branch campus faculty are remote from the main campus collections. It was puzzling to learn, however, that the main campus faculty rely more and to a significant degree on their personal collection than do branch campus faculty. Use of personal collections by researchers has been documented in other studies.[4] Perhaps branch campus faculty need to be made more aware of this apparent standard practice among researchers. Since they tend to have fewer numbers of more seasoned faculty than the main campus they simply may not have had time to develop adequate personal collections.

The branch campus faculty publications do not have significantly fewer references per article than main campus faculty. Indeed, in the case of monographic references they tend to have more. The number of references per article is not necessarily an indicator of quality, but this concern was mentioned periodically as a desirable aspect of the study and so it was investigated and a myth was shattered.

Why effective and efficient access was ranked high as a reason for faculty use of the University Libraries and ineffective and inefficient methods as reasons for not using the Libraries may not seem obvious. Since faculty estimate that half of needed material come from the Libraries, perhaps it can be assumed that *that* half they consider convenient, the other half is obtained inconveniently. Further study is needed here.

The comments received may be one of the more valuable results of the study for the Libraries. At least *these* faculty are for the most part satisfied with service and aware of library problems given academia's present economic state.

IMPLICATIONS

Although there are no standards for support of faculty research, given Penn State's collections, the faculty appear to be well served. A high percentage of materials cited in the sciences and social sciences is available for use. The humanities faculty are not as well served but given the nature of their research (reliance on unique manuscript collections, for example) these faculty do not fare all that badly. Since faculty are resourceful and take the line of least resistance working with their own collections to a fair degree, it would seem that the Libraries could serve them even better if some emphasis was given to developing collections complimentary to their own. Given faculty need to use other libraries attention should be given to developing reciprocal access and borrowing agreements while strengthening existing ones.

APPENDIX:
UNIVERSITY LIBRARIES SUPPORT OF RESEARCH
QUESTIONNAIRE

1. What percentage of the materials (books, journals, newspapers, etc.) that you have used in conducting your research over the last several years would you estimate has been obtained from collections in The Pennsylvania State University Libraries System?

   _____ %

2. Rank the items listed below from 1 (most frequent) to 6 (least frequent) corresponding to the methods or sources you use to obtain the materials needed to conduct research.

_____ a. personal collection of materials

_____ b. borrow (or use) materials from PSU Libraries

_____ c. borrow materials through PSU from non-PSU libraries on interlibrary loan

_____ d. borrow materials directly from non-PSU libraries

_____ e. visit and work in PSU libraries

_____ f. visit and work in non-PSU libraries

_____ g. other (please describe below)

3. If you assigned a *1 to items b or e above,* respond *only* to part A below. If you did *not* assign a *1 to items b or e above,* respond *only* to part B below.

    A. The factors listed below might explain your reliance on PSU Libraries for materials. Please rate *each* facor with a 1 for *major* factor, a 2 for *minor* factor, or a 3 for *no* factor.

    _____ a. The PSU Libraries collections include the materials I need.

    _____ b. The methods set up for obtaining materials from PSU Libraries are effective and efficient.

    _____ c. The collections and facilities at other libraries are not convenient for me to use.

    _____ d. I structure my research projects based upon the materials I know are available in the PSU Libraries.

    B. The factors listed below might explain your reliance on non-PSU sources for materials. Please rank *each* factor with a 1 for *major* factor, a 2 for *minor* factor, or a 3 for *no* factor.

    _____ a. I am not aware of the materials which are available in the PSU Libraries.

    _____ b. The PSU Libraries collections do not include the materials I need.

    _____ c. The methods set up for obtaining materials from PSU Libraries are too cumbersome or inefficient.

    _____ d. The collections and facilities at other libraries are more convenient for me to use.

    _____ e. My personal library contains the materials I need.

4. Have you ever modified or given up a research project because the resources you needed were unavailable in the PSU Libraries? Please check correct choice.

    Yes _____

    No _____

5. Identify the department and college to which you are presently assigned.

Department _____

College   _____

6. How many years have you been a member of the PSU faculty? _____

7. Have you ever recommended titles for addition to the collections of the PSU Libraries? Please check choice below.

Yes _____

No _____

Didn't know that I could _____

8. Your comments and recommendations on how the PSU Libraries could improve its support of your research efforts would be appreciated. Please use the back of this form.

PLEASE RETURN THE COMPLETED QUESTIONNAIRE IN THE ENCLOSED ENVELOPE BY NOVEMBER 30. THANK YOU FOR YOUR COOPERATION AND ASSISTANCE.

NOTES

1. *ARL Statistics, 1982–83* (Washington, D.C.: Association of Research Libraries, 1984).

2. James G. Neal and Barbara J. Smith. "Library Support of Faculty Research at the Branch Campuses of a Multi-Campus University," *Journal of Academic Librarianship*, 9, no. 5 (November 1983):276–280.

3. Robert N. Broadus. "Citation Analysis and Library Collection Building," in *Advances in Librarianship*, Vol. 7. Melvin J. Voight and Michael H. Harris, eds. (New York: Academic Press, 1977).

4. R. M. Fishenden. "Methods by Which Research Workers Find Information," in *International Conference on Scientific Information, Washington, D.C., November 16–21, 1958,* Vol. 1. (Washington, D.C.: National Academy of Sciences, National Research Council, 1959), pp. 163–179.

STAFF DEVELOPMENT ON A SHOESTRING

Helen Carol Jones and Ralph E. Russell

INTRODUCTION

Historically, American libraries have been concerned with development of collections and physical facilities; the development of library staffs has taken short shrift—if it received any shrift at all. Since the end of World War II, however, there has been a growing concern among organizational theorists and enlightened managers for the worker, for his self-esteem, and for the quality of the workplace. This concern has had its impact on libraries and their organizational structure. Today many libraries have translated their concern into carefully developed programs designed to provide staffs with access to a coherent and imaginative sequence of developmental activities. Indeed, there are many libraries with an administrative staff position whose re-

Advances in Library Administration and Organization, Volume 4, pages 121–131.
Copyright © 1985 by JAI Press Inc.
All rights of reproduction in any form reserved.
ISBN: 0-89232-566-6

sponsibilities include specifically the management of such a staff development program.

Unfortunately the mounting concern for the individual worker and quality of the workplace has been undermined in the present decade by the erosion of financial resources available to managers. Libraries of all sizes and types are dealing with the sobering realities of static or declining budgets and diminishing buying power of the dollars allocated for library services and collections. There is a strong temptation in the face of such realities to regard the staff development program as a dispensable frill, peripheral to the central library missions of collection development and delivery of services.

It is our view that staff development should be regarded as fundamental to the vitality of a library. Rather than permitting the staff development program to be an area vulnerable to budget cuts, we must regard it as so integral a function as to be indispensable. And it is our conviction that effective staff development does not require a large budget to hire a big name speaker or a major workshop leader; rather, it requires some creative thinking and ingenuity, careful organization and preparation, and administrative concern and support.

Staff development programs may provide skills, facilitate tasks, or provide information leading to a higher level of job expertise. They may also provide experiences which contribute to a more accurate or positive perception of oneself and the workplace. This latter is an often-overlooked but highly desirable by-product of the staff development program for many staff members. It should, in fact, be targeted as a positive goal of the program and, we feel, can hardly be over-emphasized. A positive attitude toward the institution and toward one's work in it usually translates into improved job performance.

One other factor of paramount importance should be mentioned. The administrative climate, or the attitude of the library administrators, is critical to the success or failure of any staff development program. It is not just a matter of providing resources, i.e., time, space, or funding for coffee and Cokes. While those certainly are important, the essential element is an unequivocal acknowledgment by senior management of the value and importance of the program. If staff development is to succeed in a library, management must clearly demonstrate, by actions as well as words, their concern and support for the program. Without such support, the prospect for any success in staff development efforts is limited indeed.

The impetus for this paper is a strong commitment to and concern on the part of the authors for staff development; that is, the development of *all* staff. The intent of the paper is to address the quandary of many libraries: how do we plan and implement effective staff development programs with severe limitations on resources specifically allocated for that purpose—or with no resources at all? Our paper is intended to be a generator or source of ideas rather than a research article. It is, in its purest form, a listing of low-cost activities which have worked in at least one situation and should be applicable in many types and sizes of libraries.

A primary goal of any staff development program should be to provide for each staff member a firm sense of identity in his job assignment and within the organization. The staff member should be helped to understand his individual role in the macrocosm—to understand the importance of his own work assignment and the ways in which his work interrelates with the work of others in the organization. The staff member thus informed will be more likely, for example, to understand how a breakdown in the flow of work in one department of the library can cause problems down the line for someone in another department—and to know and care about the staff member whose work is affected by his own. Moreover, the staff member who knows others on the staff by name and by job function will be less likely to experience the destructive effects of isolation and anonymity.

A reception to honor new personnel is one of the simplest yet most effective forms of staff development, one which will establish a keynote of warmth and friendliness which can carry over into later contacts among staff. The occasion should be an informal party during the work day held in the staff lounge or other appropriate place. Expense can be minimal with coffee and Cokes from library funds and a few homemade goodies donated by individuals on the staff. Repeat the occasion once a quarter— or more or less frequently as dictated by staff size and turnover rate.

A large influx of new personnel in a single department may provide the opportunity for a special staff event. Recently when

seven new staff joined our Circulation Department, the department heads of Reference and Circulation arranged a get-ac-
quainted party for the two public service units. In part as a result
of this party, the frequent daily interactions among members of
the two departments have had a more personal quality and patrons have the benefit of the two units of the library interacting
smoothly and effectively in providing service.

Another important developmental experience for new staff is
a tour of the departments and functional areas of the library,
including the library administrative office. If it is logistically possible, plan the tour so that the flow of materials in the processing
stream is evident, and then give the department head or supervisor in each unit five minutes to describe that area's mission.
The tour guide should be alert to point out relationships and con-
nections as the tour progresses. And it is a good idea to punctuate
a long tour with a rest break over coffee. As with the new staff
reception, the library tour should be a recurring event, whenever
several new staff have been employed or regularly every three
months with large staffs.

To help a staff member place his job and his library in the
larger context of the world of information, it is useful to arrange
staff tours of neighboring libraries and information facilities. In
a large metropolitan area there will be many opportunities to
enable a staff member to enlarge his understanding both of the
varied types of libraries and of changing approaches to the processing of information. In recent years our staff has visited the
new Central Library of the Atlanta Public Library system, the
Georgia Department of Archives, the libraries of the Federal Reserve Bank and the Atlanta *Constitution,* the National Library
Bindery, and the Jimmy Carter Presidential Library (still in its
formative stages). In the future it is likely the staff will visit the
facilities of the Cable News Network. While the range and variety
of libraries may be more limited in a smaller community, there
can be value in almost any well-planned visit to another library
facility, both through the increased interaction between the staffs
involved and through the resulting benchmark against which the
staff member can place his own job and library.

A second area of emphasis for staff development should be
the development of personal skills and expertise. This is an aspect
which is easy to overlook in planning the personnel development

program, perhaps because these skills have such broad application in the lives of employees beyond the limits of the library job. This, however, does not lessen the impact they can have on job performance. For example, workshops on assertiveness training, which have been so popular in recent years, can be made directly relevant to library personnel who need to develop coping skills for dealing with problem patrons. The staff member who does not realize that he can stand up to an irate library user is at a decided disadvantage and at some risk to his mental health. For a public service staff member, appropriate assertiveness is necessary for a healthy perception both of himself and of his job. Similarly, staffs can benefit from workshops focusing on time management, stress reduction, or developing communications skills. Libraries located on or near a college or university campus will usually be able to take advantage of workshops of this type offered by the campus counseling center or continuing education staff. The counseling center may even be interested in designing a workshop specifically for your staff, as in the case of the "problem patron workshop." Other libraries may need to draw on the resources of the community for workshop leaders, perhaps through contacts with the local mental health association. In some instances the workshop leader may be found within the library. However it is arranged, this valuable aspect of personnel development can be managed at minimal expense to the library.

An area of general personal development with very specific application to the library job is that of training in management and supervision. Local resources may be difficult to identify for this kind of workshop; but here, as in other areas, the larger entity of which the library is a part—university, city government, corporation—may provide the leader. If not, then ask an experienced and successful supervisor within the library to "bone up" and provide an hour or two of advice and information for interested colleagues. This experience will provide staff development for the workshop leader as well as for those listening. Make this workshop opportunity available not only to supervisors who want to sharpen their skills but also to non-supervisory staff who may wish to enhance their opportunities for promotion.

A third major area of focus for the staff development program is the development and enhancement of specific library skills and job-related expertise. This is another aspect of staff development which can be managed with little or no direct expenditure of library funds. It is limited only by the fertility of the imagination at work in the planning and by the amount of time available to be allocated for staff development.

An imaginative way to build on the introduction to the library provided by the tour for new staff is to design a bibliographic instruction session especially for support staff, emphasizing ways in which library users are making effective use of materials provided by the staff. The staff member who is new to libraries will gain a deeper comprehension of the significance of the work he does, and he may be helped to become a more effective library user himself.

All staff will benefit from a session which highlights the acquisition of a new piece of equipment or the institution of a major new service. Recently when our library acquired a Kurzweil Reading Machine for the visually impaired, the manufacturer's representative and the staff member designated to work with the machine provided an interesting demonstration with value for the entire staff. While only one individual will be working with the equipment, it is important for all staff to be aware that it is available and to understand the ways in which it is useful.

When our library acquired a large number of microfiche readers for the introduction of a COM catalog, we invited the vendor representative to provide workshop sessions for our public service staff on simple maintenance procedures and minor repairs to the equipment. A vendor representative may be eager to talk to reference staffs about new products or older ones that may be underutilized. Our reference staff has benefited from recent sessions with representatives from Congressional Information Service, Newsbank, and Information Access Corporation.

The institution of a new service should be made known to all library personnel and the participation of library personnel in the development of a service should be appropriately acknowledged. Staff throughout our library have been involved in recent months in preparation for the opening of a new law school as part of the university. Staff tours of the new facility provided an important culmination with appropriate acknowledgment of extraordinary efforts. When our reference staff instituted online searching of computerized data bases, all library personnel were invited to attend one of a series of sessions highlighting the development and application of the service and demonstrating the use of the equipment. This sort of activity not only heightens the interest and awareness of staff in the organization but also acknowledges their status as important members of the team.

Earlier in this paper we recommended the value of the staff tour of a neighboring library. This kind of tour, involving fairly sizable groups of staff and a limited time frame, is necessarily a rather superficial and fleeting developmental experience focused on enlarging the staff member's concepts of libraries and the information world. However, there is a place in the staff development program for other levels of staff contacts with neighboring libraries, providing a deeper, more intense, and better-focused experience. This can occur one-to-one between individual librarians or can involve small groups of staff or entire departments. Our reference librarians have paid half-day visits to the Reference Departments of four member libraries in our urban consortium, three nearby academic libraries and the central public library. The focus of these visits goes beyond merely getting acquainted with professional colleagues, although that is one important result. A primary goal of the visit is the sharing of information about facilities, resources, and services, particularly those that are unique to the other institution. A result is that our reference librarians are able to make patron referrals to the other libraries with greater ease and confidence. Similarly our area map librarians, documents librarians, inter-library services librarians, catalogers, collection development personnel, and library administrators benefit from the shared information and experience which comes about through the planned counterpart visit or exchange.

On still another level there is the day-long or even two- or three-day visit to a library of similar type or with interesting solutions to problems faced in your own library. This involves sending a vanload or several carloads of library personnel on a cross-country jaunt, and while it certainly cannot be accomplished without some outlay of funds, there are ways in which the expense can be minimized, and the benefits usually far outweigh the costs. The detailed examination of another library which is part of such a trip will invariably provide fresh perspectives and new insights into the policies, procedures, priorities, and even the colleagues at home. Often the "chemistry" among colleagues sharing this combination of travel and professional experience is something which could not be achieved in a day-to-day work environment. Often staff groups return from this trip with a sense of renewal and an acknowledgment that their own library is, after all, better than they had realized. A group of this kind can cut across staff lines to include supportive staff, non-supervisory librarians, and middle-management positions. It works well if the visiting staff are paired appropriately with counterpart host staff members. A venture of this magnitude, both in terms of the number of personnel involved and the expense, requires extensive and careful planning on the part of both the host library and the visitors. The benefits derived through this kind of cross-fertilization experience and the stretching of the individual beyond the limits of the particular job or library are often intangible and may not be immediately apparent, but they should not be underestimated.

Cross-fertilization or exchange programs can occur within the individual library at much less financial cost but with great benefit through increased knowledge of the procedures and activities of other departments in the library. Reference librarians may spend a half-day a week working in the Catalog Department, as they do at one of our neighboring institutions. Librarians from throughout the staff may be participants in the program of bibliographic instruction. Administrators may wish to have a closer contact with the library's patrons through an hour or two a week at a public service desk. Although this is clearly a virtually cost-free form of staff development, it does involve the cooperation of two or more department heads and the support and approval of the library administration. As with some of the other forms of activity we have mentioned, it involves a degree of risk-taking and a sense of adventure, and it can result in the loss to the library of valuable staff who have become more desirable personnel through the quality and variety of the experience they have gained.

With encouragement and support from the library administration, the personnel within a department may take responsibility for development of creative in-service training. Reference staffs are noted for this kind of activity, typically a weekly or perhaps monthly seminar series devoted to enhancing reference skills and knowledge. The seminars can be quite varied both in content and in form, and the benefits occur on several levels. Participants in the seminars are exposed to new sources, new ideas, or perhaps a review of a thorny old source such as the *IBZ (Internationale Bibliographie der Zeitschriftenliteratur);* the seminar leader has the opportunity to develop new areas of knowledge and to try out teaching skills with supportive colleagues.

From time to time our Reference Seminar Series draws on the expertise of information experts in the community. Recently our reference staff has had a valuable session on statistical publications of the Bureau of Labor Statistics given by a BLS information officer and a demonstration of online searching of the census data base by a representative of the State Data Center. This is also a suitable setting for contacts with vendor and publisher representatives. And, of course, there is no cost to the library.

If your budget is not healthy enough to send staff away to workshops, it may be possible to develop a workshop in your own community through the continuing education division of your own or a neighboring institution. If you can identify both a need and an appropriate expert to fill that need, approach the continuing education division with a proposal and offer to help with identifying the target population (local librarians) and developing the mailing list. They may reciprocate by giving your staff a reduction on registration fees. We have recently been able to make available to our staff in just this way an extremely useful workshop on grantsmanship.

Another creative way to bring the expert to your staff is to offer to be the host library for a sabbatical visit by a librarian or library school faculty member from another institution. The visiting librarians may be interested in the opportunity to work in a library for an academic term or academic year or to serve as a resource person or visiting scholar for a period of time. Advantages will accrue to both parties with such an arrangement. For the host library, the insights of the visiting scholar can be applied to operational problems. As a stimulus for staff development the individual may be invited to meet informally with library personnel as well as to make formal presentations. Probably the most significant benefits will come from the one-on-one interactions inherent in the process.

An oft-overlooked and perhaps undervalued form of staff development is the strategy session which should precede attendance at professional meetings. With the costs of travel rising and professional travel opportunities for many staff accordingly limited, it is more important than ever to develop techniques for assuring that maximum value will be derived from attendance at a meeting. A way to move toward this goal is to bring together before a planned professional meeting the seasoned professional travelers with the more novice attendees. Program in hand, they discuss approaches to dealing effectively with the conference to come, discussing the value of different types of sessions with hints to pinpoint the potentially more helpful—or least helpful meetings. This technique is particularly appropriate to meetings of ALA, where the complexity of the structure and the sheer size of the meetings can be overwhelming. It is useful as well, though, for smaller state and regional association meetings. Follow-up sessions can contribute to staff development as well, particularly if they involve a reporting session on meetings attended and a sharing of information, ideas, and news from the conference.

With the climate established by such an approach to dealing with conferences, it may be possible to encourage within the library's professional staff a network of mentoring relationships. The novice professional who is trying to penetrate for the first time the maze presented by the professional literature and professional groups may be justifiably bewildered. An experienced staff member may be willing to provide the guidance he needs. As the younger professional moves toward readiness to pursue such creative professional outlets as research, publication, or program participation at conferences, he will benefit from the intellectual stimulation and moral support as well as the role modeling derived from the seasoned mentor. The mentor may invite the junior professional to co-author a paper or to participate in preparing a grant proposal with potential benefit to both members of the relationship. The mentoring approach may be extended to department or library-wide brainstorming sessions on ideas for research and other creative projects.

While many of these activities can be found in various and sundry types of libraries across the land, the effort to rationalize or synthesize the separate parts into a logical whole may be absent. It is important to regard your staff development activities as parts of an integrated program. Further, make certain your staff perceives the various activities, particularly the more informal ones, as a planned part of a coherent whole. As a publicity technique, disseminate the full program to the staff with an annual calendar, frequent report from the staff development committee in the library newsletter, and an attractively presented annual report. The raised consciousness will enhance the value of the various program components, and the heightened awareness of the importance placed on personnel development by the library administration should provide a context for the emergence of still more creative and low-cost approaches to the staff development dilemma.

Libraries in the decade of the 1980's are faced with hard decisions. Increasingly library administrators will be forced to evaluate programs, establish priorities, and, in many instances, discontinue doing some of the things which traditionally have been considered important. We hope that we have shown that staff development programs need not be among those scrapped in the face of diminished resources. Staff development on a shoestring can be an exciting and richly rewarding enterprise.

THE IMPACT OF TECHNOLOGY ON LIBRARY BUILDINGS

Rolf Fuhlrott

INTRODUCTION

In the past, the question of the impact of technology on library buildings was answered with a simple presentation of technical facilities in library buildings. As for me, I would prefer to look into this problem from another point of view—that technology itself has made certain forms and structures possible. Yet I am quite aware of the fact that the appearance of a library is not exclusively determined by technology; the underlying concept of the library, i.e., the philosophy by which it is conceived, is also determinative. Nevertheless, I wish to examine the impact of technology in three fields: (1) construction technology, (2) building equipment, and (3) library technology.

Advances in Library Administration and Organization, Volume 4, pages 133–157.
Copyright © 1985 by JAI Press Inc.
All rights of reproduction in any form reserved.
ISBN: 0-89232-566-6

CONSTRUCTION TECHNOLOGY

As everyone knows, library buildings are storehouses for book stocks which must take into account that these stocks are steadily increasing. A building with contents subject to increase is inevitably too big at the beginning of its utilization, i.e., when first occupied; after a few years, however, often much too soon, it becomes too small. From this tension of size, librarians have begun to call for an optimal usage of buildings, guaranteeing all future requirements. Certainly the meeting of these requirements is only one aspect, though the most important one, for the construction of a library building. Further requirements are form and design, adaptability to natural surroundings, or to the town picture, workplace layout for the library staff and building regulations, all of which determine the appearance of the building. The architect has to unite these aspects into a first class whole, at the same time finding a definitive form. Consequently, a great variety of designs for a great variety of libraries exist, according to the constructional feasibilities of the various geographic areas.

With the introduction of cast iron into the building trade of the past century and the invention of concrete, constructional developments have made manifold forms and girder constructions possible. Conventional structural principles were improved by strength tests and scientific calculation methods. Structural stress analysis as well as new jointing methods offer a great variety of construction techniques, iron and later concrete allowed extreme stress due to their inherent strength.

Subsequently, new load bearing systems were developed which determined, too, the appearance of buildings, halls and rooms, often leaving the means of construction visible. Though an eighteenth century baroque library allowed a great variety of artistic creativeness, technology had not much influence on its appearance. As late as the nineteenth century, the Bibliothèque Ste. Geneviève in Paris gave an initial idea of the possibilities of iron architecture, that is, the construction of a lofty and spacious room, as was later achieved by means of the very same architecture iron in the Bibliothèque Nationale in Paris. For a long time the exterior architecture of libraries remained the same, while almost everywhere the new building material, concrete, became a sign of the times. Concrete opened new dimensions to the building trade and made creative expressiveness possible.

Liquid when poured, concrete gets its final shape when hardening in a mold, thus creating nearly unlimited possibilities for inventing again and again new constructional forms (Figure 1). Concrete provided immense stimulation for creation of new forms, some of which are, however, quite ugly.

Though no material is in itself ugly, misuse can spoil it. It has been possible to construct tall buildings, even skyscrapers, side by side without adapting them to natural surroundings, without taking the small individual buildings of the locality into consideration. Certainly the contrary is possible, too: to construct a library which dominates a town picture, even one rising above the comparatively small buildings of a university campus. "Highest" example is the 28-storied library building of the University of Massachusetts in Amherst. Though library towers are popular with many architects, they are not popular with librarians. Disadvantages of a tower building are its small base, because a relatively large part is consumed by supply ducts and other utilities etc.; departments belonging together are distributed among several floors; too few transport facilities cause long

Figure 1. The brutalism in concrete architecture shows the facade of the Robarts Research Library at the University of Toronto.

Figure 2. Reading room landscape of the State Library Preussischer

waiting times, etc. In contrast to these tower buildings, there are also large scale constructions limited to a few stories in height. Always desirable are floor areas with as few hindrances as possible, so that it is desirable to make use of built-in units or girder elements, which function as supports or walls. Area-covering structural elements can bridge large rooms, for instance, cupola or shell constructions or suspended roofs. The older libraries of London and Washington are well known for their huge domed structures, which determined their form and design. Even the appearance of modern libraries is to a large extent determined by the structure of their supporting elements. These supporting structures can be load-bearing structures as part of single-storied rooms, or a gallery or atrium. The folded plate roof of the U.S. National Library of Medicine in Bethesda, for example, makes a roof-light system possible. This illuminates the upper floor office rooms as well as the ground-floor catalog rooms. Suspended roofs come up to an extraordinary span and supply large reading rooms with light from both sides. Huge prestressed concrete girders which bear a saw-tooth roof (north-light roof), their lower ending being formed by a perforated ceiling, have created the splendor of the reading room landscape of the State Library Preussischer Kulturbesitz in Berlin (Figure 2). Daylight penetrates through the north-lights and light cupola into the room. In the evening they diffuse artificial light. During the first half of the nineteenth century, storage towers and blocks were typical, especially of German libraries (Figure 3). At the end of the nineteenth century, large quantities of the book stock were kept for reasons of economy in closed stack rooms. Early in the twentieth century, the space-saving arrangement of books according to accession number (e.g., *numerus currens)* was introduced, though after some hesitation. Because of this method of arranging books, stack rooms were developed, which have become typical of library buildings. When the idea of open-access libraries spread from the United States and Great Britain to Germany, appearances and structural systems of German libraries changed, too. Years which were marked by an economic upswing and a building boom followed. An increased demand for scientific education favored the building of new universities. Prefabricated structural designs were developed and produced at low cost, which allowed swift construction of cubical buildings by uniform planning grids.

Figure 3. Outside of the stack building of the Cologne University Library
(FRG).

Public demand left no room for architects' calls for a great variety
of designs. The combining of unpleasantly cold materials and
designs resulted in uniformity and monotony (Figure 4) of both
exterior and interior appearance. Large open-access areas became part of the planning grid of 7.20 meters. Later, in recalling
aesthetic values and artistic creativeness, many library buildings
of architectural quality have been built.

Recently concerns have arisen in regard to new building materials and construction methods. The results of research on
reinforced concrete, wooden particle boards and some plastics,
which are supposed to cause injuries to health, are still disputed,
though there is no doubt that the employment of artificial and
synthetic materials does not remain without side-effects on man's
physical and psychic comfort. In some parts of the Federal Republic of Germany, once frequently employed and low-priced
asbestos cement can no longer be used for the construction of
public buildings. Increased radioactive radiation has been noticed
in other frequently used building materials. Though air-tight and

Figure 4. Uniformity caused by prefabricated structures at the Regensburg University Library (Bavaria, FRG).

sealed windows reduce energy loss, they impede natural ventilation. Now a tendency towards use of conventional building
materials, original construction methods and less technology in
managing a building is noticed almost everywhere. It cannot be
denied that highly developed, expensive and energy saving
building equipment is necessary for entirely different structural
designs as, for instance, high-rise buildings or large-scale low
buildings.

BUILDING EQUIPMENT

Particularly in three fields the influence of building equipment
can be stated. The use of a library building requires:

1. Sufficient *illumination*
2. Adequate air conditioning, which is guaranteed by an air
    circulating system
3. Suitable *transportation facilities* for ease of accessibility.

Illumination

For illumination, the best use should be made of natural light,
if only because natural illumination involves no expense. No
problems exist as far as high-rise buildings are concerned, considering their small base and limited room depth. (For illumination, there is an interdependency between the depth of a room
and the height of windows.) The facade of the Karlsruhe University Library, for instance, makes this quite clear (Figure 5).
The windows of the administration rooms, with a depth of about
16 feet, have a height of about 6.5 feet, the public rooms below
have larger window areas, while the stack rooms above, with
their function of preserving books, do not have more than small
strip-line windows. In buildings like these, with a division of
functions (reading—administration—storing), it is quite easy to
differentiate lighting requirements.

Our modern libraries, however, do cause some difficulties because of their various functions: a compromise between daylight
illumination for the readers, on the one hand, and the protection
of books from daylight, on the other, can be achieved by small
strip windows (Figure 6). In such libraries, with room dimensions

Figure 5. Facade of the Karlsruhe University Library (FRG).

coming near the limits laid down by fire regulations, exclusive daylight illumination won't be sufficient. For that reason, reading and book storing areas are separated from each other again. Daylight areas will serve for reading, possibly aided by indoor potted plants for comfort's sake (Figure 7), while the interior is reserved for the book stock, thus making artificial illumination necessary. This interior "book area" is sometimes two-storied, thus achieving twice the room height and a larger room depth for daylight illumination.

A better and constant room illumination is achieved, if daylight enters from above. North-light roofs and roof superstructures

Figure 6.   East facade of the Freiburg University Library (FRG) with the small strip windows.

allow illumination independent of the room depth. All light openings, however, require shading devices against harmful radiation. Sun protective devices should stop sunbeams, glare and heat, but at the same time guarantee a view outside and air conditioning. They should be quite easy to install, to use and to maintain; durable; and at the same time low priced. There is no device like that which comes up to all these requirements of course, so one has to find a compromise. Reflection, absorption and dispersion of sunbeams should take place outside a building, since an inside shading device heats the window panes and consequently the adjacent area. Mobile outside shading devices usually are slatted roller blinds and jalousies. Fixed shading devices are, for instance, cantilevered roofs, balconies and other projecting elements (Figure 8). Some of the standard equipment is antisun glass usually consisting of a two-piece insulating glass with the outer pane tinted, thus making use of absorption and reflection for sunshading. Disadvantages, however, will make themselves felt in winter, when solar radiation supporting room heating is lacking. Frosted glass is only employed for sky lights. In addition there are phototropic panes, used for light-sensitive glass. Their

Figure 7. Foyer with indoor plants in the Regenstein Library of the University of Chicago.

Figure 8.   York University Library in Toronto with projecting upper floors
to shade the lower ones.

purchase would involve considerable expense, so a large-scale
employment is not practical now.

Using daylight illumination determines the structural design;
artificial lighting, however, needs no further structural considerations. The fact is in the past most buildings and also library
buildings were planned without taking artificial lighting as an essential part of the design into consideration. Most times illumination was added as late as when the building was already completed, resulting in monotonous and undecorated rooms. The
illumination system should on the contrary support the architectural design in meeting functional, human, visual and biological
requirements. Artificial illumination is closely connected with
air-circulating systems, since any artificial lighting produces heat
requiring removal or transformation.

Air Conditioning

Air conditioning does not essentially influence the appearance
of libraries, apart from a few where air conditioning ducts are

Figure 9. Air conditioning ducts used for interior design at the Siegen University Library (FRG).

used for interior decoration (Figure 9). Usually, the people working in the library hardly notice the internal air-circulating system, which has made spacious rooms, as they have been designed during the past 20 years, possible. Air conditioning meets a double function: providing for human comfort by balancing natural ventilation and preserving the library's book stock.

With use of modern building materials and construction methods, buildings have lost some of their solidity in the course of years. Since the building cannot protect itself against influences of heat and cooling any more, air-circulating systems had to be used to provide this. As a result of recent repeated crises in the oil industry, dependence on air conditioning installations is going to be reduced. We know that human comfort can be achieved positively by means of construction methods. Less window area, shading devices in summer, permeation of heat radiation in winter (Figure 10), adequate insulation and smaller rooms, allowing natural ventilation, are only some ways of energy-saving building methods, which will serve human comfort.

On the other hand, air conditioning for the library's book stock,

Figure 10. Sunshading of the glass facade by planting in summer and penetration of sunbeams in winter at the Baden State Library in Karlsuhe (FRG).

does raise a lot of questions: books and manuscripts consist chiefly of organic substances which are quickly harmed by the influence of temperature, humidity, light, and pollution. It has been discovered that a 5°C reduction of temperature would lengthen the life of a book 50%. A high room temperature and high humidity speed up the emergence of microbiological parasites. Air pollution, especially with a high percentage of sulfur dioxide, is instrumental in the destruction of the library stock. Librarians have only gradually begun to perceive the danger in its whole extent, which is of alarming proportions. U.S. research institutes have discovered, for instance, that one-third of the Library of Congress' stock is already in an advanced stage of deterioration.

For this reason, the future employment of air conditioning systems will be of utmost importance, especially at archival libraries. Since the requirements for people and books cannot be lumped together, a renewed, intensified separation of reading and book-storing areas may be recommended, such as has long been the case in Europe, especially in Germany.

Transportation/Passenger Traffic

To reach the several floors of a building, there are, as there are in libraries, stairs, elevators, and escalators. Since their dimensions and safety rules are standardized, librarians have no influence on their appearance, at best on their size and number. In connection with the expansion of entrance halls during the past years, architects have been able to redesign staircase layouts (Figure 11). As to passenger elevators, librarians must insist that they should not be hidden in some corner, but located in the interest of adequate accessibility, in the library's entrance hall. Oddly enough there are no escalators in German libraries, but they are quite often found in other countries, for example, in Canada, the United States, and the Netherlands (Figure 12). Though escalators are more space consuming than lifts, they have a higher conveying capacity and can even be used as stairs when out of order. People do prefer escalators, as an investigation by a German department store chain has shown: regardless of the equal number of stairs, elevators and escalators available, the stairs were only used by 2 percent of the passengers, lifts by 8 percent, but 90 percent used

Figure 11. The open atrium in the Metropolitan Library in Toronto.

the escalators. A possible explanation could be the annoying waiting times at the passenger elevators.

LIBRARY TECHNOLOGY

Book Conveying System

The conveyance of books is of great importance to libraries especially to storage libraries. At the same time, the book transport forms a connection between construction technology and library technology, which consists of all technical facilities of a library serving the library stock, i.e. book binding and photocopying department, mechanical conveying and storing. The first

Figure 12. Moving stairs in the City Library of Rotterdam (NL).

two have nearly no influence on the design of a library, the latter does have some influence. Still the influence of book transportation needs has been declining during recent years. Large scale open access areas at ground level permit users to help themselves to the books, so there is no need of a mechanized transport system, which is why a lot of U.S. libraries lack any book-conveying system. If an increasing number of books is now going to be shelved in closed stacks, perhaps mechanical conveying will gain some importance again. Systems which are most frequently employed are conveyor belts, box conveyors and self-moving conveyor systems. Conveyor belts are used nearly exclusively for horizontal transportation and are employed to cover the distance between stacks and circulation desk. Users do not come in contact with them. Box conveyors with a load carrying capacity of up to about 30 pounds serve for vertical transport and run mostly in vertical shafts. Self-moving containers, which are provided with an electric motor and run on special tracks (Figure 13), are the most variable, thus adapting easily to changing requirements. Problems regarding the construction of all these systems rise in connection with fire protection and noise insulation. Like every building, library buildings are divided into fire compartments according to the respective local fire regulations. Between the single compartments openings are required, with closures meeting fire regulations, thus often entailing a complicated mechanism. Its opening and closing frequently involves the nuisance of considerable noise which requires insulation for it and the noise of the conveyor system. Other conveyor systems, for instance those to transport call slips or messages, have nearly no influence on the building. Still, it has to be considered that the flexibility of rooms is little influenced by input and output.

Mechanical Storing

Certainly, the influence of mechanical storing on the library building is much greater than that of mechanical conveying. The method of shelving books is known to every librarian. Shelves are either made of wood or of steel or a combination of both materials. Though steel is resistant against outside influences, there is the disadvantage of condensation, a problem being now increasingly considered by curators. The water absorptive ca-

Figure 13. Self-moving containers (Telelift).

Figure 14. Integrated lighting system on the uprights of the shelves (manufacturer Schulz, Speyer, FRG).

pacity of wood, however, has the advantage of being moisture controlling. For reasons of style, wood is used a lot today, for instance in public rooms where shelves are used for interior decoration. Free arrangement of shelves favors individual interior designs. For expediency, the distances between girders should form a whole number multiple of the shelves' unit spacing. (Several standard module sizes exist, the choice depending on the planned size of the library or its function.) In this part of the library building, librarians pay special attention to flexibility; mobile shelf systems have been developed, which frequently include integrated lighting systems (Figure 14).

Figure 15. Manually operated mobile shelves.

The storing of books in special rooms, i.e., stacks, may, as we have already seen, determine the exterior appearance of a library. Inside the stacks, books are kept in shelves standing mostly on the floor. Multitier, self-supporting shelves have the disadvantage of being fixed in one position, thus allowing no subsequent alteration. Shelves on the floor are more variable, especially if they are mobile stacks (forming so-called compact shelving), which are operated mechanically (Figure 15) or electrically.

A forerunner of compact shelving is the parallel roller cases of the Radcliffe Camera in Oxford, (GB), where the shelves can be pulled out into the aisle like chests in a pharmacy. Other examples of compact shelving are to be found in industrial storing: multi-tier stacks and revolving shelving have already been used at some libraries. As to revolving shelves, which are sometimes multi-storied, the single shelves are passing along erecting platforms at the front side (Figure 16), where books can be taken out and reshelved again. Revolving shelves are suitable for compact shelving of little-used book stock. Certainly, this system can be automated, too, if the books are kept in small containers with machine-sensitive coding and the manually-operated erecting platform is replaced by an automatic unloading and supplying mechanism. But that already belongs to automatic storing and conveying systems like "Randtriever" or "Conserv-a-trieve" units which are already in operation at a number of libraries. Here, too, the books are kept in coded containers, though in

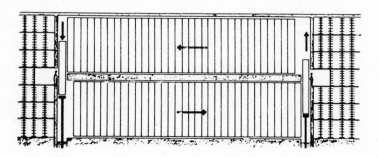

Figure 16.   Revolving shelving, the most compact system, in a seven story
stack.

fixed multi-tier stacks. Robots move between them, taking out and replacing the single containers, transporting them to the front side of the shelves, from which they are carried to the circulation desk by means of another conveyor system. This form of storing saves costs for lighting, cleaning and heating. What is more, the possibility of cold storage, since nobody is working in the stacks, favors the conservation of the library stock.

FINAL OBSERVATIONS

We have again reached a degree of library mechanization which determined both theory and practice of many librarians during the 1970s. Recently, some librarians have begun to change their views, and a tendency leading away from technology—if not even a certain hostility towards technology—has made itself felt. The latest designs for new library buildings have already shown first effects: attempts to do without air-conditioning systems and consideration of conventional building methods; increased insulation of buildings; use of less glass; sunshading of glass areas in summer by exterior planting of deciduous shrubs and trees, thus guaranteeing the penetration of sunbeams in winter; partitioning of rooms into smaller units; reduction of large free-access areas in favor of new stack rooms; daylight and natural ventilation by creating inner courts with green areas. Perhaps the reduction of library mechanization will lead to more human comfort in library buildings, giving man the feeling of determining and commanding the degree of technology and not being controlled by it. This development goes hand in hand with a present architectural trend; that is, the tendency towards international comformity seems to have been curbed and replaced by nostalgia, regionalism and individualism. A newly developed awareness of history and a revival of historical traditions will help to create distinct regional designs which, in accordance with the new library philosophy, will possibly lead away from the monotony and uniformity of many libraries toward naturally developed forms, a harmonious style and human comfort—to put it briefly, to a human architecture (Figure 17).

Figure 17. Harmonious style and human comfort in the College Library of the Federal Unemployment Office of Manneheim (FRG).

REFERENCES

Baur-Heinhold, Margarete. *Schoene Alte Bibliotheken* (Beautiful Ancient Libraries). Muenchen: Callwey, 1972.

Draper, James D. and James L. Brooks. *Interior Design for Libraries*. Chicago: ALA, 1979.

Fuhlrott, Rolf. "Geschichtliche Entwicklung der Innenausstattung von Bibliotheken" (Historical Development of Interior Layout and Equipment of Libraries). Pp. 99–122 in *Bibliotheken Bauen und Fuehren*. New York: Saur, 1983.

Fuhlrott, Rolf and Michael Dewe, eds. *Library Interior Layout and Design*. New York: Saur, 1982. (IFLA Publications 24.)

Fuhlrott, Rolf, Gerhard Liebers, and Franz Heinrich Philipp, eds. *Bibliotheksneubauten in der Bundesrepublik Deutschland* 1963–1982. (New Library Buildings in the Federal Republic of Germany 1963–1983). Frankfurt: Klostermann, 1983.

Kroller, Franz. "Auswirkungen der Klimatisierung auf die Lebensdauer von Buechern" (The Impact of Air Conditioning on the Durability of Books). *ABI Technik*, 3, no. 2 (1983):149–152.

Kron, Joan and Suzanne Siesin. *High Tech: The Industrial Style and Source Book for the Home*. New York: Totter, 1973.

Liebers, Gerhard, ed. *Bibliotheksneubauten in der Bundesrepublik Deutschland* (New Library Buildings in the Federal Republic of Germany). Frankfurt: Klostermann, 1968.

Meyer-Bohe, Walter. *Transportsysteme im Hochbau* (Transportation Systems in Buildings). Stuttgart: Koch, 1982.

Pierce, William S. *Furnishing the Library Interior*. New York: Dekker, 1980.

Poole, Frazer G., ed. "Library Furniture and Furnishings." *Library Trends*, 13, no. 4 1965):385–516.

Schweigler, Peter. *Einrichtung und Technische Ausstattung von Bibliotheken* (Furnishing and Technical Equipment of Libraries). Wiesbaden: Reichert, 1977. (Elemente des Buch und Bibliothekswesens, 4.)

WHITHER THE BOOK?

CONSIDERATIONS FOR LIBRARY PLANNING
IN THE AGE OF ELECTRONICS

Roscoe Rouse, Jr.

We live in a very stimulating time for professional librarians. You can be glad, or you can be sad about it. If you are of an adventurous nature you are enjoying your job; if you prefer the quiet soberness of the stereotyped library of yore you are a square peg in a round hole. One cannot simply drift with the tide in today's exciting information business, and that is what it is today: the information business; and no day is the same as the day before.

With the rapid thrust of the traditional book-oriented library into the space-age milieu come many, many problems, only one of which is a design for a library building that will accommodate

Advances in Library Administration and Organization, Volume 4, pages 159–175.
Copyright © 1985 by JAI Press Inc.
All rights of reproduction in any form reserved.
ISBN: 0-89232-566-6

160 ROSCOE ROUSE, JR.

the new technology in adequate fashion. The changes we see moving in upon us, brought about by new developments in laser technology; miniaturization; satellite transmission; computer progress; electronic databases; definitely will alter the manner in which we carry out our work as librarians, and will certainly have an effect upon the library building design. However, they will not change the purpose, the raison d'être, of libraries. Goals will be achieved through other means than before, and the buildings to house these functions must be planned differently than before.

How different will the architectural plans be? To what extent will the new technology affect library planning? This paper will doubtless provide no absolute and undebatable answers to those questions. We hope to present here evidence that should be given consideration when planning libraries for the future. In a sense, we are setting out to prove that library planning had best set for itself a new course. Too many of us who devise plans for library buildings that will last a century fail to try to imagine what libraries will be like throughout the century. Of course, it is impossible to know exactly, but there are signs today that were not there, say, thirty years ago. We can see trends which should properly frighten us into studying every facet of the future of the book as we know it today.

This is not to suggest that we should take as our script such fantasies as *Star Wars, Buck Rogers,* or *Star Trek,* but I wonder if that level of thinking might be better than just planning a library in the same way that we planned it 30 years ago.

The permanence, or impermanence, of library materials, i.e., books, journals, microfilm, is a key factor in the matter under discussion today. It cannot be called the most important factor because, if technology so dictates, the contents of paper printed materials would find its way to machine-readable text, regardless of the durability of paper and books. But it is an important consideration because, obviously, those who would attempt to preserve books must assuredly believe that *book* libraries will be around for another century, at least. And there is considerable interest in preserving the book.

The gravity of the matter of book and paper longevity is borne out in the literature. The Council on Library Resources in New York made a survey of U.S. Book publishers through its

Committee on Production Guidelines for Book Longevity and learned that nearly two-thirds of a relatively small number of respondents use acid-free paper for some or all of their books.[1] Of the small number responding to the survey, 72 out of 111 already use acid-free sheets for at least some of their books. CLR is making an effort to influence publishers to use long-lived paper through their study of the matter, the use of surveys, and other means.

The American Library Association (ALA) has approved the formation in recent years of committees and sections concerned with book and paper preservation, some of which are now active in conducting programs on these issues at national conferences. At the ALA annual conference in Los Angeles in June 1983, the Buildings and Equipment Section presented a program titled "Optimum Library Environment for Books and People: How to Achieve It." The purpose of this program was to present the various means utilized in the construction and renovation of library buildings to control the environment in which library materials are placed so that their life will be extended. Speakers included three architects who had either planned the construction of a new facility or renovated an older facility—in each case designing buildings that incorporated the latest techniques for the preservation of materials—and a paper conservationist. Areas of concern included architectural considerations to prolong the life of materials, as, for example, covering large pane glass windows with special material which serves to screen out the ultraviolet rays deemed harmful to paper and film.

A handout at the ALA's BES program was an extract from the "RLG Preservation Manual," December 1982 draft. The paper, titled "Environmental Control for Library Collections," is issued by the Research Libraries Group. It details requirements for microforms and paper as temperature, relative humidity, air movement, protection from light, fire, and water.

The Public Libraries Division of the American Library Association has a unit titled Preservation of Library Materials Section. This unit joined with the Buildings and Equipment Section to sponsor the program described above.

In the Association of Research Libraries, there is a Preservation Planning Program—a new preservation microfilming component of the ARL Microform Project—and other programs presenting preservation techniques that are currently available. The interest in these programs and activities attest to the importance of preservation issues to the ARL membership. The Association of Research Libraries', Five-Year-Plan has, as its number 3 objective, the following: "To increase the number of member libraries engaged in programs to preserve their collections."

Another major effort in the preservation arena is the receipt of a $1.35 million grant by the Research Libraries Group (RLG) from the National Endowment for the Humanities and the Andrew W. Mellon Foundation for a cooperative microfilming project in which seven RLG libraries will participate. The project focuses on monographs, U.S. imprints, and Americana, published between 1876 and 1900. Most of these publications appeared initially on highly acidic paper.

On April 29, 1983, the Library of Congress presented a program titled "Library Preservation: the Administrative Challenge." Sixteen speakers outlined the presentation priorities facing research libraries and suggested specific management approaches for incorporating preservation into library organization and operations.

The Library of Congress has recently produced a 51-minute videotape which provides information on paper-making processes, the problems of deterioration, solutions through mass deacidification including the experiment for deacidification of 5,000 books at the Goddard Spaceflight Center; and ongoing pilot projects to use laser optical disk technology for preservation and resource access. Copies of the film are available for loan through the National Preservation Program Office at the Library of Congress, or may be purchased for $75.

The American National Standards Committee Z-39, Library and Information Sciences and Related Publishing Practices, has issued the draft of a paper on "Permanent Paper for Library Materials." The paper describes the need for a standard which will establish the criteria for permanent uncoated paper, that is, paper which will last at least several hundred years without significant deterioration under normal library use and optimal storage conditions. Actual observations and laboratory test results show that paper meeting the standards for pH and alkaline reserve described in the draft will survive just as the paper made in the fourteenth and fifteenth centuries has survived to the present day.

All the efforts and programs described here to preserve today's library materials, be it paper or film format, imply that librarians are striving for assurance that the codex will be extant for many, many years to come—perhaps, centuries. There appears to be no capitulation on their part to the possible supremacy and inevitability of machine-readable textual material and its replacement of the hand-held bound book. Nonetheless, librarians are moving forward unrelentingly in their search for faster, more comprehensive and less laborious information dissemination techniques and, through modern technology, they have been successful in finding it. Data base searches involving Boolean logic are commonplace. Some publishers now issue, in machine-readable format, the publications they once issued as traditional books or journals. Whether this process will be adopted on a wide enough scale to virtually remove books as the most common tool in the library, and thereby seriously influence library construction, is not yet known, but these are "straws in the wind."

Despite phenomenal scientific advancement in all areas of our civilization over the past one hundred years, no change has occurred in the climates in which we dwell—the environments which definitely influence the way we build our libraries. There has been, in fact, increased degradation in the quality of air due to dispersing into it large quantities of pollutants on a daily basis. We experience the same destructive storms as those of a hundred years ago—hurricanes, floods, tornadoes, typhoons—and the identical heat and drought, the same enemy of paper—humidity. Man has not diminished these potentially dangerous powers in the slightest. We are continually plagued by the same destructive vermin as were the enemies of libraries one hundred years ago—the silverfish, termites, bookworms, and their like. Perhaps one hundred years from now these same climatic conditions will exist and these same vermin will still be with us.

The spring 1983 meeting of the Association of Research Libraries, held in Banff, Alberta, Canada, carried the theme "Research Libraries in the Online Environment." The conference has been termed "a blend of practical information and speculation on the impact of the online environment on research libraries and the issues that will have to be faced in the future." As a member in attendance I found the presentations relevant, intriguing, challenging, and even somewhat intimidating.

Among the topics discussed which portent change of vast proportions in our libraries and in the planning of our buildings were alternatives currently available for communicating data: satellites, broadcast cable, and fiber optics. Several trends were noted toward increasing miniaturization, higher speed transmission at lower cost, dense off-line storage at lower cost, increasing potential for decentralization of creation of and access to data, and continuing shifts in the relative cost advantages of choices of technologies. One presentation dealt with the rapid and relatively inexpensive sharing of data by libraries, information transfer and various networking configurations, including utility-based networks (e.g., cable for audiovisual and textual service, electronic mail/messaging services, document delivery) and multipurpose networks that combine functions such as word processing, database searching and manipulation, and gateway—or intelligent network—services that provide access to online data in different formats.

The Five-Year Plan, drafted by the Association of Research Libraries in April 1983, includes a statement to the effect that "the mission of the Association is to strengthen and extend the capacities of its member libraries to provide access to recorded knowledge. . .[and] to make scholarly communication more effective."[2] The document makes reference to "changes in publishing patterns, in communications and data storage technologies." It is noted that the Association wishes to have these changes "tracked and their effect on research library service. . .analyzed and thoroughly understood." An example of the actions ARL might take in this regard was, as stated in the paper, "an examination of alternative ways for libraries and universities to identify, acquire and provide access to electronic publications when they become generally available in the next few years."

Michael Gorman wrote in 1982 "my unequivocal prediction is that by the end of the decade, the majority of American libraries of all kinds will be involved in, or affected in a major way by, online catalog systems, i.e., most libraries will allow direct access by means of computer terminals to detailed bibliographic and status information about their collections."[3] Gorman continues in the opinion that some librarians believe "that the online catalog will not arrive or, if it does arrive, will constitute a relatively minor technological change. The latter school believes that the change to an online catalog is comparable with the significant-in-the-short-term but ultimately-trivial change from a card to a microform catalog. Such a view is profoundly mistaken. The online catalog will be at once the greatest symbol of change, the greatest instrument of change, and the greatest result of the revolution in libraries of these latter years. . . .Online catalog [data bases] will reflect the holdings of a number of libraries. Electronic union catalogs will transcend the limitations of library physical plants and the parochialism those limitations have fostered." Gorman continues with the premise that online catalogs will materially affect many aspects of library operations, and he names specifically reference, bibliographic instruction, organization and management, resource sharing, and of course technical processing. Each of these will in turn have an effect upon the finances of the library, says Gorman. I will take his premise further and project that a domino effect will be felt throughout the library including space utilization.

Alfred Bork of the University of California at Irvine authored an article titled "Books versus Computers-Learning Media" which was published in the *Proceedings of the 43rd ASIS Annual Meeting, 1980.*[4] Bork contends that the new technology will displace, at least to some degree, the book as we know it today as a learning tool. "The book is the dominant delivery mechanism for learning today without question. Even where other modes such as lectures are important, in schools and universities, the book is still the most important learning mode. If we leave these formal institutions and look at the bulk of the students' learning, books constitute the major tool available. Remember that the book is a relatively recent learning device, considered against man's history; it is only within the past 500 years that books were possible and only in about half that time that books were widely used in the learning process. . .but now there is a challenger, the computer. The computer, while very little used in learning environments at the present time, shows great potential particularly in dealing with just the two problems raised. The contention of this paper is that we are on the verge of a major change in the way people learn. . . .I intend to present the evidence that such a change is about to occur." Bork explained that one of the major advantages of the book is familiarity, and pointed out that during the first year of experiments which he conducted, students were offered a choice between computer and non-computer approaches to a beginning physics course. He said three-quarters of the students selected the non-computer approach. "This number has changed in each of the years we have offered it," said Bork. "Now three years later the percentages have reversed with three-fourths of the people picking the computer approach."

The author points out some computer advantages, including that of interactivity and individualization. The learning process can be an active experience for every individual, with the computer engaging in a conversation with the student, constantly asking the student to respond, to do something, to play an active role in the learning process. He said this is to be contrasted with books, which for many readers are very passive learning devices. As to the costs, Bork noted the relatively lesser cost of printed materials at the present time, but pointed out the rate at which they are increasing and the trend toward lower costs for computer equipment and software. He said, "the future is with the computer."

The author's final comments point to the role that both the computer and the book play in the learning process. His opinion is that both will continue to be used. "A likely scenario for the future is that books and computers will both be used often together, but it should be clear from my comments that the relative advantages of computers in mass education will become more and more apparent. The problems of mass education and the problems of different backgrounds will be more and more met by the computer rather than by the book. So we will see over twenty-five years, a transition from one dominant learning medium to another dominant learning medium, a transition that does not occur often in human history."

Six years ago a publication was issued which purported to tell us something about libraries in the twenty-first century. Edited by Herbert Poole, the book is titled *Academic Libraries by the Year 2000; Essays Honoring Jerrold Orne.*[5] It is my opinion that the book is, largely, a disappointment if one reads it through to gain a feeling of the setting in which academic libraries will be found in the year 2000. One writer in the volume, Virgil Massman, discussed an interesting document issued by the U.S. National Commision on Libraries and Information Science ad hoc subcommittee on the Probable Impact on Economic and Technological Trends. Among some very stimulating ideas to come from this committee is the "synoptic" journal, he said, where full text will be delivered on demand. Indeed, at the present time a page of text can be transmitted in six minutes or less by telecopies on commercial telephone-connected equipment. As the band width is expanded, it may be feasible to send a page of text not only cross-country but around the world in fractions of seconds and at a low cost. Massman speaks of the buildings of the future to a limited extent, noting that there will be continuing efforts to limit the size of libraries.

The Deputy Librarian of Congress, William J. Welsh, wrote also in this book of the potential offered in future years by the refinement of the technology for libraries. He tells us about: reading from the television screen at home; optical storage now being less expensive than magnetic tape in large-scale; read-only applications; television transmission from microformats (a reality in some banks at present); and microfiche documents stored locally or moved by satellite transmission. Now we are facing the reality of the existence of these technologies which represent significant developments with which we, as librarians and library building planners, must deal in the very near future, if not at present.

Electronic publishing is a catchy phrase. It is a stimulating idea which excites the sporting blood in us. Those who like challenge and wish to conquer new frontiers will be interested in this new technology. It is further proof that the life of the librarian can be adventurous and exciting. But one must be free of "future-phobia" and anticipate years of exciting possibilities ahead to venture into this strange new world.

We are not talking about things to be, or inventions in the development stage. We have with us today disk-like communication media that yield moving pictures as well as sounds, television screens, and instantaneous information sources where once we sought out the reference book. Even Roger Tory Peterson's avian knowledge and his proven popularity with bird watchers is in the process of electronic publication through Houghton Mifflin. Random House is now publishing softwares which they distribute to educational institutions to be used in Radio Shack computers.[6]

Computer typesetting which has been around for more than 20 years has matured sufficiently to allow the *Academic American Encyclopedia,* in its 21 volumes, to be composed on the computer and appear in machine-readable form. Released in 1980, this encyclopedia can be accessed online through OCLC, Inc., and other data bases. We have other examples, of course, including Bowker's *Books in Print,* out of which have arisen twenty publications of other sorts.

A survey of electronic publishing would be immediately out of date because it is impossible to cite all projects in progress at any one time. The field is highly volatile, moving at a rapid pace around the world.

Harper & Row has plans for a data base in 60 different industries whereby directories will be published by geographical area—all industries, for instance, in Japan, or Germany, or England.

"Like many other publishers, we're looking at the ways we can distribute our data by nontraditional means," says David Weaver, a vice-president of McGraw-Hill, a company which has developed films and video cassettes for training programs in data processing and management.

Educators are embracing the machines warmly enough to encourage Scholastic Incorporated—which calls itself "the nation's largest publisher of educational periodicals for students in grades K–12"—to start up a new magazine, *Electronic Learning.* Scholastic estimates that educational hardware will be a billion dollar business within the decade.

A report on a two-day conference on "The Print Publisher in an Electronic World," held in December 1980 in New York, notes that the conference drew more than 300 executives from publishing companies, as well as from industries concerned with telecommunications; advertising; research; government and education.[7] They came hungry for hints on how to profit from the new technology, the report said, "and from the outset the strategy for book publishers seemed clear. Publishers have the information software and in the years to come, sports and cultural events and movies won't suffice to keep the electronic media supplied with material so publishers' wares will be in demand."

One speaker, Michael Dann, referred his listeners to Alvin Tof-
fler's *The Third Wave* for an analysis of the new era we are en-
tering and cautioned them that the electronic revolution of the
eighties involves major changes in lifestyle. "What's happening
now," in Dann's view, "is lots bigger than whether the book
will remain in its present form." People are changing not only
the way they get things but also what they want to get. Mr. Dann
said that in his opinion the average family in the United States
will spend $1,000 a month or more on electronic gear and pro-
gramming for the home by the mid–1980s. (As a member of what
I think is the average U.S. family, I do not agree with Mr. Dann
as to the high dollar figure he chooses to use.)

The Reader's Digest Association has acquired a commercial
data base retrieval service called The Source. The data base offers all manner of factual material: United Press International
Files; more than 4,000 extracts from the *New York Times* Consumer Database; employment openings registered with Career
Network; restaurant guides; etc. The Source has attracted some
9,000 subscribers so far and some forecasters expect this number
to be around 20,000 in the near future. Each pays a $100 one-
time membership fee and the charge thereafter is $15 per hour
for use of the system from 7 A.M. to 6 P.M. Monday through
Friday and $4.25 an hour at all other times and holidays. It is
possible to access The Source from any computer, no matter
how dumb, a company representative says. It is available to 230
metropolitan areas through a local telephone call.

The Source is one example of the means by which our registered library users will seek information, as the glamour and
excitement of information retrieved via such unique means
catches on, and surely as it becomes reduced in cost through
volume use.

In 1981, *The Drexel Library Quarterly* devoted its fall issue to
considerations of electronic delivery of information, giving that
publication the title "The Electronic Library."[8] Edited by Kenneth Dowlin, Director of the Pike's Peak Library District in Colorado Springs, Colorado, the publication includes contributions
by noted individuals writing on the computer and what it can do
(Joseph R. Matthews); electronic delivery of information (Richard
T. Sweeney); future information delivery systems (Brigitt Ken-
ney); Networking and the Electronic Library (Neal Kaske and

Nancy Sanders). Some quotations from this publication point up the opinion held by some, that electronics will dominate our libraries sooner than we think:

> We live in an ever-changing world and in order to thrive and even exist we must change with it. The field of library and information service is no stagnant backwater in our society. It promises to be a driving force as we move to the post-industrial age (Kenneth Dowlin).
>
> Today we are continuously being exposed to the marvels of a variety of new technologies. . . . Video disks, two-way interactive cable television, satellite television, electronic mail, personal computers, word processors, fiber optics, computer-based telephones, and teleconferencing are among the technologies being discussed (Joseph R. Matthews).
>
> *Business Week* in June 1981 predicted that 8,000,000 U.S. homes will be linked with computer data banks by 1990. . . . American Express predicted that 8,000,000 U.S. households will be using home terminals by 1985, five years earlier than *Business Week* predicted. . . . Clearly, industry is preparing for the spread of the home terminal information-retrieval systems and the public library must do likewise (Richard T. Sweeney).
>
> Electronic publishing which will produce information only in digital formats, will perhaps be one of the most heavily felt influences in the library's role in storing and retrieving information. If journals, technical reports, patents and the like are available in electronic form only, how will libraries store this material? Or will they? Perhaps they will only provide access to remote databases containing such material. Two encyclopedias have already been made available in electronic form; handbooks and other reference works are sure to follow. This can mean that libraries would either have to have their own large electronic storage and retrieval facility or would need to be tied to regional or national "electronic reference centers" where librarians and clients could search the desired database. . . . Libraries will cease to be *places* and instead will be organizations of people, working at home much of the time, and providing the expertise necessary to help users with the confusing variety of differing and competing technologies, and with searching and retrieving the many electronic data stores throughout the U.S., and, eventually, the world (Brigitt L. Kenney).

In a telephone conversation the writer had with Kenneth Dowlin in July 1983, he was asked to describe the library building which he would plan to serve clientele 50 years from today. His first response was that the building must be flexible as great change will come within that 50-year period. He had no doubt but that books as we know them today will still be here but in smaller numbers. He calls it the best "knowledge instrument" known at this time but cautioned that because it takes two years to create a book, much information will be needed long before it can be published in book format. Reference tools will need to be transposed into machine-readable data first, and that is now taking place. Periodicals will be early among the types of materials offered in machine-readable format, especially in scientific fields. Dowlin calls for a building with "tons of power" as, he notes, we have always outstripped the power supply in the buildings we plan.

Dowlin remarked on the service patterns of library buildings and the way they fluctuate through the years. He commented on a 1957 building which he occupied with a total of 86,000 square feet and only two offices. He said there is a great need for more office space because of the change in job assignments which have taken place over the years. He points out the need to move from communal space to private work space, although that work space need not be enclosed by walls.

Dowlin sees a need to provide power and communication cables through drop ceilings and "power poles" rather than through floors or walls. His experiment with a "raceway" was not successful. He asks for a service tower from the basement to the roof with power and communication lines housed therein. Cables could be taken from the tower and run through any ceiling within the building.

In years past Dowlin worked with a "core" which served the building for housing personnel, stairways, and utilitarian purposes. His future building, he says, will not utilize the core in the center of the building since it can get in the way and all movement must be around the core.

Asked whether he would predict that most of the book collection would be stored away in a less accessible area of the building, his response was negative, noting the fact that he directs a regional public library rather than a research library. He would still ask for shelves and browsing areas in his building. The library director noted that with the cost of books going up and the cost of electronic access to information coming down, it is inevitable that we will see fewer books added to our collections and more electronic software purchased in the future.

In another direct telephone inquiry made at the same time it was learned that *Encyclopaedia Britannica* is producing software packages of programs in areas of mathematical science; language arts; special education; living skills; and vocational education. This data can be accessed on home or school computers. I was told that *Encyclopaedia Britannica* has no plans at present to put its entire publication online.

It seems evident that numerous innovations are yet on the drawing boards and there will be challenges untold ahead of us. Unquestionably, the profession must look to the future with the hope that a new generation of "mixed technology specialists" will be prepared to carry on library service traditions.

Educational Facilities Laboratory (EFL) was founded in New York in 1958 by the Ford Foundation for the purpose of conducting research and experiments in educational facilities. In the late 1960s, EFL called together a group of people knowledgeable in higher education, in academic library management and in architecture. They were asked to consider whether, at that point in time, academic library planning was meeting the challenge that the future might hold for academic institutions. The question put to the gathering was: should library buildings of the future be designed primarily for the printed book? A week later the group submitted its report to the organization's president. They had reached the conclusion that academic library planners were, for the most part, projecting their thinking into the future and that, indeed, the codex book will be the mainstay for library building planning for the foreseeable future. That meeting was held about 15 years ago. In view of the changes in information transfer technology over that fifteen-year period, were I in a position to do so, I would call for another such conference and ask the same question again. The factors with which the participants would work today would, indeed, be quite different from those of 1968.

Considering the large number of libraries which have already installed computer equipment, it hardly seems necessary for us to discourse on site preparation, specifications and plans for such equipment. This is part and parcel of library planning today, without question, or, at least, I certainly hope it is. There are numerous places where one can find this kind of information in today's library planning literature and it will not be explored here today.

TALMIS is the acronym for Technology-Assisted Learning Market Information Service, an organization concerned with the use of microcomputer software and interactive video materials for training and education. In 1980, the organization held a conference in Chicago called "Interfacing Industry Components" attended by 200 participants representing a broad mix of traditional educational publishers; audiovisual producers; computer software publishers; computer retailers; computer hardware manufacturers; and educators.[9] Discussion sessions ranged from software publishing ventures to the use of computers for educational purposes. An electronic publishing consultant who reported on the conference noted that "documentation—the book that accompanies the software program—is a very important part of electronic publishing. Software is the exciting wave of the future, but books are the rudder; publishers have an important role in keeping these new products on an even keel." He further reports that the discussion seemed to underscore the fact that "there are no established answers in this young and experimental field."

Richard M. Dougherty, writing about the impact that networking has on library management, mentions the managerial implications of computer-produced products, noting that their emergence has already generated a plethora of practical and philosophical issues.[10] Dougherty says, "There is every reason to believe that today's generation of computer-based services is only the harbinger of greater changes to come."

The new technologies which have found their way into libraries are bringing a need for a new kind of planning. The design for a new library building should be screened much more carefully than in the past. While we cannot accurately predict the exact needs of libraries 50 years hence, we should at least let our imaginations run rampant and be prepared for the worst—or best. In some cases, the arrangements in a completed building for electronic and automated devices will not be evident in a casual visit to the building, but in the ceilings, floors and walls will be practical provisions ensconced for future needs, much as one fills a time capsule for opening on a specific date far in the future. Careful planning will assure future information scientists (librarians, if you will) of adequate power distribution (and I emphasize *distribution);* floor loads; heating; ventilating; air conditioning; air purification; sunlight screening; and arrangements for complete flexibility. As Elaine and Aaron Cohen have said in their book, *Automation, Space Management, and Productivity*, "In a technological age, space management is not an afterthought."

Some will assume that we cannot, today, plan practically and viably 50 years ahead for a technology which is developing as rapidly as our computers; electronic devices; lasers; satellite transmissions; and miniaturization. Truly, we cannot be precise in our planning and we will surely err in some ways. At the very least, however, we should, in my opinion, make an effort to provide for growth and inventiveness in these areas the best that we can.

When we have qualms about the so-called bookless society, we should stop to recall that the codex came into being at the cost of sheepskin scrolls, and they at the cost of clay tablets. We may find it hard to visualize but I would lay a bet, if the fact could be proved, that many an Alexandrian scoffed at the new-found sheepskin scrolls, probably accusing them of being short-lived. Likewise, I think many a monk accustomed to reading from scrolls held only disdain for cut pages bound into codex form.

The advancement and progress to come belongs to no one in particular; it is mine, it is yours. We can prepare for that future as we so desire and I believe we have an obligation to think; to ponder; to dream; to visualize; to plan; to hope; so that the goal will be defined. This generation of librarians, architects and library building planners can even set the wheels in motion toward the Never, Never Land of what has been unfortunately termed "the bookless society." Most of us think of that term as a defamation, but it really is not so; it does not describe a society of low intellect, watching only soap operas on a television screen. But because we cut our teeth on books; learned from them; abide by them; swear by them; love them; we cannot tolerate anything called "bookless." I, personally, doubt that we shall ever be "bookless."

Let us take up the challenge thrust upon us by the new technology to prepare for that boundless and interesting future of serving up "reading materials" in whatever format to an information-hungry populace. We can plan better buildings and give better service than ever before.

NOTES

1. *CLR Recent Developments* (September 1982) : 3.
2. ARL, "5-Year Plan" (April 14, 1983) : 2.
3. Michael Gorman, "Thinking the Unthinkable; a Synergetic Profession," *American Libraries* (July/August 1982) : 473.
4. American Society for Information Science. *Communicating Information* (New York: ASIS, 1980) : 13–16.
5. Herbert Poole, *Academic Libraries by the Year 2000* (New York: Bowker, 1977).
6. Robert Dahlin, "Watch That Book!" *Publishers Weekly* (March 20, 1981) : 24–30.
7. Judith Appelbaum, "Looking at the Problems," *Publishers Weekly* (March 20, 1981) : 26–27.
8. *Drexel Library Quarterly* (Fall 1981).
9. Sharmon J. Hilfinger, "Educational Publishers Explore Electronic Future," *Publishers Weekly,* (March 20, 1981) : 12–13.
10. Richard M. Dougherty, "The Impact of Networking on Library Management," *College and Research Libraries* (January 1978) : 15–19.

ATTEMPTING TO AUTOMATE:
LESSONS LEARNED OVER FIVE YEARS AT
THE PITTSBURGH REGIONAL LIBRARY
CENTER

Scott Bruntjen and Sylvia D. Hall

INTRODUCTION

Most advertisements for microcomputers feature the executive beside the highlighted system making the single masterful key stroke which, with the response it provides, saves the organization from oblivion. The desk is clean, there are no wires in evidence, the furniture is tasteful and all in view are smiling. Such a concept is possible but there is a tremendous amount of effort required before such a condition can be reached.

What follows describes one organization's effort over the last five years to reach that utopia presented in many system ad-

Advances in Library Administration and Organization, Volume 4, pages 177–192.

vertisements. Along the path a number of lessons were learned and often relearned. These lessons as presented are designed to generalize this one experience to that applicable to many small organizations.

BACKGROUND

In the last 15 years librarians like the operators of other small businesses have had the opportunity to race through five generations of computer support. Those who entered the profession in the late 1960s have seen batch processes on mainframes, minicomputers with poorly designed data bases attempting to support circulation control activities, microcomputers which were employed to support games, a beginning attempt at sophistication in both software and data base development, and a recent and remarkable explosion in the support library administrative and technical operations in the form of incredibly powerful microcomputers. This article is a case study of the lessons learned in the development and initiation of one such microcomputer system.

In late 1982 the Pittsburgh Regional Library Center (PRLC) was awarded a contract by the State Library of Pennsylvania to design a complete administratve support microcomputer system and to distribute it to libraries of all types throughout the State. During this effort to bring computer support to libraries, PRLC examined the lessons it had learned as it had worked to automate its own internal operations.

To put the lessons learned in this five-year experience in context one needs to review the background of PRLC. The PRLC was organized formally in 1967 with the dual missions of cost savings and resource sharing for libraries in the city of Pittsburgh. From the original nine institutional members in 1967 The Center had grown to more than 50 members by 1979 when the organization had its first brush with in-house computer support.

STANDALONE WORD PROCESSING

With a skeptical Board but armed with a consultant's report and $17,000 in grant money PRLC purchased what it believed that it required: standalone word processing in the form of a Lanier "No Problem" word processor. The structure of PRLC at that time was a small office staff of five who were required to produce an incredible amount of repetitive information in the form of letters, mailing lists, accounting documents, and reports. The tasks of the organization were focused on the coordination of the activities of member institutions and in the administration of a contract with the Online Computer Library Center (OCLC).

What was understood was that with a growing membership and with a static-sized staff, the organization required the type of office automation that could serve as the tool to help, through the automation of routinization and repetitiveness. What was not understood was that the organization and, indeed, its consultant should have examined the then-current and future automation tasks that would have to be performed.

That Lanier of 1979 is for sale today; and the price of a new replacement machine has decreased from the more than $20,000 actually expended to less than $5,000. In one way it was a good purchase for it provided the much-needed local automation education that the staff of PRLC required as they began to help their member libraries deal with similar automation questions in the years that followed. That Lanier was excellent for data entry. Its training programs and documentation were, for its day, fairly complete and well designed but it had minimal processing capability. It could not work effectively with text more than one page in length for it treated each page as a separate file. Modifying a sentence on a one-page letter worked, but the addition of a paragraph on a page one so that text was moved to a page two was not the easiest task.

But that equipment served the initial purpose. It permitted the organization to grow without the addition of more staff, and the products that were produced looked better and were produced faster than had been possible with the two electric typewriters that were its predecessors.

Within half a year PRLC had the opportunity to purchase two dial access terminals; one, a video device and the other, a printer. With the lessons learned from the Lanier purchase, which was still being forcefed to some staff who preferred to stick with the typewriter and white-out, PRLC took the position that the funds for those two terminals might be better expended on a microcomputer. The search from that microcomputer was comical in retrospect but is illustrative of some basic points.

With the Lanier word processor providing the daily word processing, albeit in what is considered an archaic manner today, the staff moved in two directions. First, they approached the Lanier sales force with the requirement of two additional types of software: what would now be called a "spreadsheet," and communications capability. The sales force although friendly, was unable to understand the basic question. Lanier was able to provide a program called "Math Master with Snap" which facilitated arithmetical functions on columns of numbers and a communications hardware and program package which made the Lanier capable of minimal communications with other devices and data bases. The mathematical functions were added, but the communications portion investigated was dropped as a dead end.

FIRST MICROCOMPUTER SUPPORT ATTEMPTS

The second path of investigation proved more fruitful. Still knowing little, PRLC looked at the retail outlets that were just beginning to support microcomputers. The first examination was of an Apple. Again PRLC found the sales personnel friendly, but not knowledgeable, and the equipment of minimal capability. Random Access Memory (RAM) sizes were at the level of 4K. Screen displays had capabilities of 40 columns uppercase only. No standard peripheral interfaces were available without the expensive addition of boards and ports. Support, in most cases, consisted of printed literature.

With that discouraging attempt, PRLC began a serious examination of the performance capabilities it wanted for the resources that it had available. It is interesting to note in retrospect that this was the first point at which an investigation of the specifications required had taken place. Later experience with bringing truly powerful automation to many smaller organizations found that this same route featuring a lack of specifications was followed by many. This examination of the alternatives included a number of systems with the eventual purchase in 1981 of a North Star Horizon equipped with communications capability;

word processing through Wordstar (a software program that provides file- rather than page-oriented text management); a programming language; a minimal dot matrix printer; and a not well designed (for today's standards) video display unit with keyboard.

PRLC did not know what it had in this package in the way of capability. What it thought it had was a more flexible and powerful word processor than was present in the Lanier—the ability to support some minimal programming in Basic, and the ability to communicate as a terminal with external data bases. All of that was true, yet it was but a scratch on the surface.

Nevertheless, the organization made only minimal use of the equipment for the ensuing six months. The word processor, although extremely more powerful than the capability present in the Lanier, was not well organized for data entry. The printer that came with the system produced barely legible text. The documentation was written by engineers and programmers for others of similar background. The communication capability was certainly present but no separate telephone line had been installed, consequently everything was executed in an ad hoc manner.

This was the high point of the Lanier and the poor initiation of the North Star. The Lanier, though limited as it was in computer power and software, was organized to fit into an office. Data entry was simple and the directions were fairly well written. The staff who had taken time to accustom themselves to the equipment were now beginning to use it as a tool rather than as a mere curiosity. The North Star was abandoned for several months in the press to get other tasks accomplished.

In early 1982 the staff maximized the Lanier through the design of a comprehensvie program that developed an organization data base; produced mailing labels; kept track of certain accounting and use statistics; produced a membership directory; invoices; membership letters; and all of the other recurring reports that surround the operation of a membership organization. The task of creating that complete software proved a good learning experience for the staff and it brought to light some of the inadequacies of the equipment.

That standalone word processor was pushed to the limit. It took more than three hours to sort a hundred-item data base for the preparation of the membership directory. If it failed in the last few seconds of that sort—which happened with regularity—

the work had to be begun all over again. It could add figures—but it could not deal with missing values and persistently put in zeros. The staff renamed the Math Master with Snap software—"Math Master with Snip"—as they manually erased all of those extraneous zeros prior to sending invoices.

The Lanier had its problems, but so did the more general microcomputer. The Horizon was an 8-bit, 56K RAM machine with both serial and parallel ports. The printer was minimal but it could change print sizes—albeit with great difficulty. The word processing program used multiple key strokes rather than cursor arrows, to move around the screen; and the CRT was not designed for either data entry or long use. The entire situation was further deteriorated by the fact that any change in the configuration was difficult at best. No single cable could be purchased that would connect the two printers. The installation of the word processing program for any new CRT or printer, required an expert. The documentation was designed for someone who already knew the answer.

The Lanier came as a self-contained workstation with the well-designed keyboard at typing height. The North Star with a standalone data entry device was wherever someone put it. Nevertheless, this was the end of the Lanier-style generation, and the beginning of the supplanting of such equipment by more general-purpose microcomputers.

With those functional specifications that the staff had attempted to develop for the microcomputer came also a requirement for software with more capability. During the time period of 1981—1983 came a tremendous response by both hardware and software vendors. The first library of software that PRLC developed was approached in as haphazard a way as its first purchase of office automation. To microcomputer word processing was added the ability to check spelling; sort lists; merge standard paragraphs into letters; use an online thesaursus; produce automatic indexes and tables of contents; and to keep all of these documents in a data base.

Software vendors in particular had begun to take what were well-written programs and to add to them intelligible documentation and training programs. The original Horizon was moved, by PRLC to a standalone application in the area of computer tape management and was replaced in the office environment with a much-improved North Star Advantage. This new equipment provided a keyboard and screen more than equal to the well-designed Lanier. It used an enhanced version of Word Star that utilized cursor control arrows and preset function keys that greatly simplified data entry. Its documentation was so written that an answer could be found by someone who did not already know the answer, and it permitted use of all of the software packages that had already been purchased for the older Horizon model.

With the first Advantage—a two floppy disk drive, 8-bit, 64K RAM machine with excellent graphics—the organization finally had equipment equal to all of the best points of the Lanier but with infinitely more capability. Yet still there were serious limitations. The spelling program, for example, required continual switching of three disks so that the program of 20,000 words could be run against the the document to be examined. The Horizon and the Advantage used the same floppy disks—but they could not communicate directly. The only communication devices that either had were 300-baud (approximately 30 characters per second) modems. More seriously, both were limited in the number of characters that could be kept in permanent storage. This limit to the file size of a diskette meant that any large data base would have to be designed in approximately 300,000 character increments. While far superior to the older standalone word processor, it was not adequate to proper support of office automation.

For much of 1982 the organization took a number of false steps. It investigated and purchased several accounting packages; all, however, designed for "for-profit" organizations. Each such system forced the difference between revenue and expenditure into owner equity rather than into excess of revenue over/under expenditures. None dealt well with multiple funds. All were very expensive but ineffective. In almost every case the software could be examined in the detail necessary only after purchase. Payroll programs were unable to deal with the Pennsylvania requirement for tax-sheltered annuities (from federal tax) to be taxed at the state level. A lot of software was purchased but at minimal organizational value. The Lanier continued to support repetitive forms production but this use for it began to decrease.

In addition to software false starts, the organization took time to move on to the level of being able to input a significant amount of information to permanent storage in the computer itself. As part of a separate tape management project—which was by the summer of 1982 running in an experimental mode with the Horizon as its base—PRLC purchased its first hard disk. This device could hold 18 million characters in storage and could access any of those characters through the Horizon to which it was connected. That 18-Mb (megabyte) hard disk weighed about 60 pounds, was almost three feet long, and cost about $6,000.

The concept was to use the hard disk to store bibliographic information that would be extracted from tape through software produced locally. It was soon discovered that a second tape drive—to serve as the device to store those extracted records—would be more feasible. So the 18-Mb hard disk was then connected to a second Horizon to be used to support the organization's developing data base. While the tape management operation was working a standalone function, the office automation became more confused than ever.

Present were a Lanier, still producing certain documents with ease in operator-training but with minimal capability, a Horizon with an 18-Mb hard disk, and an Advantage with two floppy disk drives. There was a lot of learning but little coordinated effort. This situation was to continue for the next year.

Staff who had learned to operate the Lanier were reluctant to change to a new machine. The Advantage and the Horizon could exchange disks, but the hard disk was technically difficult to install initially. As usual, there was little time to sit down, plan, install, train, and run an automated system parallel to the still-dominant manual systems.

With a few exceptions there were no hardware failures. The North Star equipment required virtually no maintenance and the organization elected not to purchase maintenance contracts on any of that equipment. It did have maintenance on the Lanier and it was serviced a number of times. Those few North Star exceptions, however, seemed to come at the most inopportune times. With any system failure, the loss of information was always the most critical piece. The organization had not addressed the appropriate backup procedures. With such failures the staff lost confidence in the equipment to perform as a useful tool.

Beginning in 1979 with the staff's first attempt to attach a printer to OCLC, PRLC had experienced the usual frustration of any novice user in interfacing hardware and software. The staff found out that one cannot expect to take a standard cable and plug it into a standard outlet on one machine and plug the other end into another machine and expect it all to work. The number of possibilities present with this type of computer equipment, however, seem to be endless. That first OCLC/printer experience followed the staff through the next several years as new printers, modems, and other peripheral devices were required and attached, after much frustration, to the microcomputers that were available in the office. But there was learning.

By mid-1983 it was obvious to PRLC that an overall plan was needed if office automation was to be successful. Such planning might seem obvious and simple, but it was not and it is not today, due to several factors. PRLC, as any office, institution or library, is an ongoing operation. It cannot close down for two months while the perfect solution is put in place. And the computer field is anything but stable. The right answer in any plan often becomes obsolete before it is even implemented: prices keep dropping; capabilities keep increasing; new capabilities and lower costs generate new horizons of what could be accomplished; and users are never satisfied. PRLC itself was growing. From the beginning of this effort until late 1983 the PRLC staff had increased from 5 to 35 and the funds handled had increased from $650,000 to more than $3 million while the membership had doubled.

Unlike a number of other areas there were few members of the staff who could help, for there was no one with three decades of microcomputer experience just as there had not been any microcomputers for three decades. The several computer generations—from mainframe support from an outside source through the early tools, like the Lanier, to the tools in place, or at least in use, by 1983—represented a tremendous change in less than four years. And so it was time, by summer 1983, to either plan or fail. Any planning had to incorporate the lessons that had been learned to date and had to include in the configuration all of the components already available as there would be no new large resources to start over.

A PLANNED MICROCOMPUTER SYSTEM

In the late summer of 1983 the following tenets of a plan were adopted. First, there were some actions that would probably operate best if they remained standalone separate operations. Second, some fixed point had to be adopted for a level of capability that could be maximized even though it meant that the answer would not be state of the art at all times. In a larger organization, perhaps, new improvements could replace older systems configurations but in a smaller organization one had to set certain requirements and then stick with them until a very measurable rationale could show that a change would be useful. Third, no matter what the impact on the current operation, certain implementations had to be made on a schedule as established—or the organization would never make progress. Finally, the system as adopted had to present as much standardization and flexibility as possible so that the organization could take advantage of some increases in capability. While the organization was limited in resources, it had as its mission to continue to stay near the state of the art so that it could help its member institutions make use of increased capabilities in like systems. It is to this last question—the requirement to progress and to use limited resources while at the same time staying as current as possible for education purposes—that made the planning especially difficult.

The system being designed, finally, was one that was to be functional, supportive, and at the same time, illustrative of the newest capability. For all of these reasons, the PRLC staff chose a multi-system plan. The components of this total system were as described below; a standalone tape-management system, but with the ability to integrate the tape units and the bibliographic records that the staff had been able to manipulate into other parts of the system; a Local Area Network (LAN) of North Star Advantages to support all of the office automation issues that had been present from the beginning; a multiuser IBM compatible North Star product, the Dimension, to provide a training facility and double as a data-entry facility.

The office automation which had been operating on, it is fair to say, a hodgepodge of equipment, with uncontrolled files, was to migrate to a single system of standalone microcomputers, each of which could function separately but which could also communicate via LAN. The LAN facility provides the ability for each separate processor to send files to shared devices such as printers or modems; it permits files to be transferred from machine to machine; and it supports an intra-office electronic mail facility.

The network as designed and implemented in mid-1984 consisted of eight North Star Advantages. These machines were located on three floors of an 8,000-square-foot office. Four of these Advantages were hard disk models which gave the network a total of 50 megabytes (50 million characters) of storage, in addition to the floppy disks that could run locally at each station.

The network had available to it two letter-quality printers, a 1,200-baud modem connection to a dedicated telephone line, two graphic printers, a 600-line-per-minute line printer, a color printer, and a plotter. Common software in the network included a complete word-processing package including dictionary, thesaurus, mailing list program, sort program, data base manager, two graphics programs, several spreadsheet programs, a statistics package, a communications package, and other similar general software. The concept was that from any of the eight workstations a user could sign on; check for intraoffice mail; use any word-processing, statistics, graphics, etc. package resident in the network control hard disk; design specific output; and send that output either via modem to another organization or to any of the specialized printers.

To facilitate the use of the office automation system certain actions were taken. The two remaining typewriters in the organization were moved to difficult-to-use locations. There are times when a typewriter is the most efficient method of production but those times are limited and this technique forced all users to use the computer equipment. Rather than "orange crates" for workstations, the equipment was placed at proper typing-height, set up as complete workstations. Local software was available to be kept by each user, but there was a minimum need to do that given the shareable software kept by the system. Operating manuals were purchased in multiple copies so that each user would have the documentation needed to use the system.

With a change in personnel, the one position in the organization holding the designation "secretary" was eliminated and replaced by a telephone receptionist, a part-time microcomputer trainer and a cleaning service. The financial resources that had gone to support a secretary thus were put to eliminating environmental disruptions so that managers and technicians could spend more time in production. The Lanier was put up for sale and in the meantime removed from operation.

While not enough time has passed to determine if this LAN experiment was successful, there are some early evaluations of it. The staff that had shared the previous full-time secretary found that it was far simpler to produce their own finished correspondence on the system than it had been to dictate, modify, and produce correspondence with the assistance of a secretary. The resources that could be redirected—to someone to coordinate and screen telephone calls; to someone who could perform building maintenance services; to someone who could provide a training base, to a system trouble-shooting service—all came from the eliminated position that had provided merely typing support. This solution has been found to be most beneficial.

Needless to say, the system did not install itself; threading the cable through three floors of an old building; connecting equipment that none of the staff had ever seen before; and designing the files to be held centrally, and the files to be held locally, took time. But the resulting increase in productivity was well worth the effort. The PRLC organization could have determined that it wanted all IBM-PCs connected through a similar network, but it took as two basic provisos the utilization of already present software, all of which was 8-bit, configured for the North Star and the satisfaction with the speed of the 8-bit machine, over the faster but more costly (given the resources already expended) 16-bit next-generation equipment. As a basic premise in this situation, PRLC accepted the screen filling a little slower, or sorting taking a little longer, as a trade-off against the inability to use the already present components.

REINFORCING THE LESSONS LEARNED

PRLC has a major mission of training libraries in the use of new automation support. Under a grant from the State Library of

Pennsylvania, PRLC spent much of the fall and winter of 1983 selecting, installing, and training librarians on an IBM lookalike—the Columbia Data Products microcomputer. Much of what the organization had already learned was applicable in that task, as it set out to install microcomputers in more than fifty libraries in its region.

It soon discovered that training was of paramount importance if libraries were to use the equipment that had just been installed under this grant. For that reason, PRLC used some of the funding that had been saved, by replacing the secretarial position with office automation to hire a part-time microcomputer training-and-support-manager. While the initial training was done at each library's site, it became evident that special group training at PRLC was essential for the advancement of the effort.

Rather than use standalone computers for training, the PRLC automation plan was enlarged to include a training facility that would be equipped along the lines of a language lab. The concept was that each student would have a separate workstation, but that each would be connected to a central machine which could emulate the IBM-PC, or the Columbia, and which could use the same software that had been distributed to the libraries as part of the grant. Individual work could then be monitored by the instructor who would have the added ability to project by a video device to a large screen from that of a particular student, when such an example would be benefical to the class as a whole.

Consequently, the second element of the PRLC automation plan became the acquisition of the North Star Dimension. This equipment in brief had the ability to replicate the capabilities and functions of 12 IBM-PCXTs simultaneously with the ability of each workstation to access shared peripheral devices such as printers or hard disks. Thus students could use familiar software and a familiar keyboard, but in an environment in which each workstation could be put in place for less than a quarter of the cost of a standalone Columbia or IBM.

This training-manager had the following responsibilities: working with each of the libraries via field visits and telephone; designing and implementing training; installing; troubleshooting; training the PRLC staff in the use of the office automation support system. While the Dimension and the Advantage network could not access each other directly, files could be shared via a modem transfer, and certain peripheral devices could be shared via intelligent switch boxes. The most important connection, however, was the training manager who had expertise on both systems.

A 12-station multiuser, multitasking system sitting idle, however, is a wasted resource. PRLC has had, for the last several years, the task of facilitating the production of machine-readable records in a standard machine-readable cataloging (MARC) format. Up until the time of the installation of the Dimension system, all of that conversion of records had been done through the OCLC system, and by spring 1984 the organization was using 9 terminals connected directly to the OCLC system to convert in excess of 50,000 records per month. While the OCLC conversion unit was the most efficient method to produce full MARC records for libraries, some smaller libraries could not afford the service.

The experience with MARC gained in the tape management effort; the experience with conversion gained through work with a number of libraries over the past several years; the experience with microcomputers in the production of some limited catalogs; the needs of these smaller libraries—all finally brought about a new use for the Dimension multiuser system when it was not being employed for training.

In a project initiated with one of PRLC's software engineers in spring 1984, the organization began to plan for the conversion of what was initially termed "shell MARC" records. The concept, although a complex programming question, was essentially the creation of a MARC record through data entry of the data elements present on the shelf lists of the libraries which requested this service. The software prompted the operator to enter the data on the shelf list into a software program that then recreated the MARC structure, stored the record, and later transmitted the record to the PRLC tape unit which, using an IBM-compatible computer, read the record onto an output tape. That tape of the cataloging of the library was in standard MARC II format which was as able to load into a local system as any record that might have been produced with a bibliographic utility such as OCLC or RLIN (Research Library Information Network).

The Dimension, with its 12 workstations, served as a natural data entry device. Because it was locally controlled and because the system architecture of the Dimension places a separate processor with RAM at each work station, response time is incredibly fast. The time that was lost in more keying of each record was made up by the elimination of searching and slow response time. Because there was no connection in the arena to OCLC and hence no differential charges for "prime" and "nonprime" time, the same data entry operators that worked at night on OCLC could work in the daytime on the local system. The initial pricing that was done found that records of this type which had fewer data elements, and which did not display holding symbols nationally, could be produced for about one third the cost of PRLC's OCLC conversion. The two products were different, but each had a type of library that benefited from each service.

THE LESSONS LEARNED

From that first Lanier standalone word processor, PRLC advanced in four years to three computer systems which had office automation, training, data base creation, and tape management capabilities. All of the work was done with a minimal expenditure of resources estimated at a total $90,000 one-time costs with no ongoing maintenance contract costs and actual maintenance costs of about $4,000 per year. Much of that equipment had been provided under one grant or another, and the concept from the beginning had been to maximize the resources available at present with no continuing costs.

While it had been achieved with minimal financial costs, there had been a toll on the staff. From that toll some lessons were learned. Those 7 lessons are as follows:

1. Without unlimited financial, personnel, and time resources, an organization can never expect to remain at or near the state of the art in computer support and must accept periods of computer obsolescence if it is to ever move forward.

2. Planning is essential, but an organization that meanwhile is supporting a parallel ongoing operation will not do enough of it.

3. Users will be slow to replace the status quo no matter how inefficient it may be.

4. Training is an essential and ongoing requirement; proper training requires a plan, a skilled trainer, and accurate and complete documentation.

5. Few nationally accepted standards exist in support of this type of automation. This fact increases the likelihood that there will be selection of systems without a future.

6. Acquisition of absolutely complete computer systems, including software, hardware, installation, training, documentation, and supplies, remove several levels of initial frustration.

7. The integration of computer support into the office is much more likely to be accepted by staff if it is accompanied by appropriate furniture, supply storage, and a concurrent removal of the system it is designed to replace.

SUMMARY

These initial lessons have been learned by PRLC, but the task of implementation of automation in support of daily operations is only in its initial stages. With the rapid changes in capabilities of such local and now affordable processing, improvements that such support can provide will probably never be completed. There will likely always be increased productivity improvements that can be made, although the first jump taken is admittedly the largest.

The flexibility created by adherence to standards, or quasi-standards, where they exist, the application of good systems procedures such as planning, and the willingness never to accept the status quo, can permit an organization to do more with less while even enjoying the experience. But the lack of any of these standard-, planning-, or willingness-components will cause automation to produce nothing more than frustration, unhappiness, and inefficiency. An opportunity such as this type of local, affordable processing provides is well worth taking but it cannot be achieved automatically.

ANNOTATED BIBLIOGRAPHY OF MATERIALS ON ACADEMIC LIBRARY SERVICE TO DISABLED STUDENTS, 1978–1983

Rashelle Schlessinger Karp

Most of the articles and books listed in this bibliography were published between the years of 1978 and 1983. The few that were published before these years were included because they were considered too valuable to leave out. The bibliography was constructed through a literature search of the following indexes: Library Literature, ERIC, Dissertation Abstracts, LISA, and CIJE.

Accessibility: Designing Buildings for the Needs of Handicapped Persons. Washington, D.C.: Library of Congress National Library Service for the Blind and Physically Handicapped, 1979.

Advances in Library Administration and Organization, Volume 4, pages 193–218.
Copyright © 1985 by JAI Press Inc.
All rights of reproduction in any form reserved.
ISBN: 0-89232-566-6

Annotated bibliography of books, articles, reports and films on barrier-free design for disabled persons.

Allen, Kenneth W. and Frazer, Gary. "Providing Mediated Services for the Handicapped—A Community College Learning Resources Center Perspective," *Illinois Libraries* 59(September, 1977):500–503.

Describes a special program called WHIP (Waubonsee Hearing Impaired Program) at the Waubonsee Community College in Sugar Grove, Illinois.

American Library Association. Association of Specialized and Cooperative Library Agencies. *Standards of Service for the Library of Congress Network of Libraries for the Blind and Physically Handicapped.* Chicago: ALA, 1979.

Text of the Standards.

American Library Association. Association of Specialized and Cooperative Library Agencies. Standards for Library Service to the Deaf Subcommittee. "Techniques for Library Service to the Deaf and Hard of Hearing," *Interface* 4(Fall 1981):2–3.

Discusses how libraries can serve hearing-impaired individuals. Provides guidance to all types of libraries in the areas of communication, resources, publicity, programs, and staffing. First step toward standards for library services to the deaf.

Ames, Jan. "Libraries Serving Handicapped Users Share Resources," *Catholic Library World* 52(February 1981):297–300.

Agencies throughout the country braille and tape materials to meet local needs of disabled patrons not met by the basic collection of the NLS. Cooperative activities among libraries as well as resources available to facilitate these activities are detailed.

Application of Technology to Handicapped Individuals: Process, Problems, and Progress: a Joint Report Prepared for the Subcommittee on Science, Research, and Technology. . . . Washington, D.C.: Library of Congress. Congressional Research Service. Science Policy Research Division, 1980.

Discusses the application of 5 technologies to disabled persons: information resources, educational, rehabilitation, communications, and environmental facilities. Includes bibliography and legislative considerations.

Attitudes Toward Handicapped People, Past and Present. Washington, D.C.: Library of Congress National Library Service for the Blind and Physically Handicapped, 1980.

Annotated bibliography of books, periodical articles, films and bibliographies about attitudes toward disabled persons.

Bardellini, Susan and Hartman, Rhonda C. *Higher Education and the Handicapped: Resource Directory, 1982–1983.* American Council on Education, Washington, D.C. HEATH/Closer Look Resource Center, 1982. ERIC Doc. No. ED 224 201.

Includes an analysis of the Rehabilitation Act of 1973 (Section 504), a listing of Section 504 Technical Assistance staff in 10 regional offices, a listing of agencies helpful in resolving issues regarding disabled college students, and a bibliography of publications on accessibility, resources, disabilities, and employment.

Baskin, Barbara H. and Harris, Karen H. *The Mainstreamed Library.* Chicago: American Library Association, 1982.

A compilation of articles that deal with three questions: what are the issues that librarians must confront to meet the challenges posed by mainstreaming; what changes in policies and practices must be made; and how can traditional services be modified, broadened, or replaced to meet the special needs of this population. Includes discussion of physical accessibility, materials selection, technology, computers, and outreach programs.

Bauman, Mary Kinsey. *Blindness, Visual Impairment, Deaf-Blindness: an Annotated Listing of the Literature, 1953–75.* Pennsylvania: Temple University Press, 1976.

An annotated bibliography of nonmedical, mostly monographic literature about blindness, visual impairment and related topics. The bibliography is periodically updated in the journal, *Blindness, Visual Impairment, Deaf Blindness: Semiannual Listing of Current Literature.*

Begg, Robert. "Disabled Libraries: an Examination of Physical and Attitudinal Barriers to Handicapped Library Users," *Law Library Journal* 72(Summer 1979):513–525.

Begins with a brief summary of legislation pertaining to handicapped access. Professional responsibilities toward accessibility are covered, as well as specifics of physical and attitudinal accessibility. The accompanying bibliography is very helpful.

Benedict, Marjorie. *Library Signs and the Disabled.* ERIC Doc. No. ED 221 162, 1979.

An excellent, brief essay which outlines general criteria for evaluating sign systems for disabled library patrons. An instrument for the evaluation of sign systems is included in the text which points out specific design considerations such as minimum lettering sizes for different kinds of signs, mounting specifications, and optimum color contrasts.

Bentzen, Billie Louise. "Orientation Maps for Visually Impaired Persons," *Journal of Visual Impairment and Blindness* 71(May 1977):193–96.

Describes research into the design and commercial reproduction of tactile maps to the Boston, Massachusetts area.

Bliss, James C. and Moore, Mary W. "The Optacon Reading System," *Education of the Visually Handicapped* 7(May 1975):33–39.

Describes the historical development of the Optacon and how it works. Includes a bibliography of independent evaluations of the machine.

Bookmark 39(Fall 1981): entire issue.

The entire issue is devoted to library services and resources for and about disabled patrons. In addition to articles specifically about academic library services and resources, other articles detail research, equipment and general resources available.

Bopp, Richard E. "Periodicals for the Disabled: Their Importance as Information Sources," *The Serials Librarian* 5(Winter 1980):61–70.

Annotated listing of periodical literature published by and/or for disabled persons.

Bopp, Richard E. "Rehabilitation Literature: a Guide to Selection Materials," *Library Resources and Technical Services* 25(July/September 1981):228–243.

Describes and evaluates various selection tools on the basis of their coverage of rehabilitation literature and their usefulness to academic, public, and special librarians.

Bopp, Richard E. "Physically Disabled People, Personal Narratives: a Review of Recent Works," *Reference Services Review* 10(Spring 1982):45–48.

An annotated list of recently published personal narratives by physically disabled persons.

"Braille and Large-Type Publishers" in *Library Resources Market Place*. New York: R. R. Bowker Company, published periodically.

Listing of companies and associations which produce books, periodicals or newpapers in braille and large type formats or on records, audiotapes, and audiocassettes. Includes addresses and telephone numbers of vendors.

Building a Library Collection on Blindness and Physical Handicaps; Basic Materials and Resource. Washington, D.C.: Library of Congress National Library Service for the Blind and Physically handicapped, 1981.

A listing of materials recommended to libraries and organizations as basic resources for the provision of current information services on visual and physical disabilities. The list is divided by subject, and is updated quarterly in the publication, *Added Entries* (published by the Library of Congress National Library Service for the Blind and Physically Handicapped).

Carlisle, Richard F. et al. *Evaluation of Community College Handicapped Student Services Programs: a Handbook*. California Community Colleges. Sacramento. Office of the Chancellor, 1980. ERIC Doc. No. ED 184 637.

Provides general information and operational suggestions for planning and implementing evaluation of community college handicapped student programs and services. Includes bibliography, sample evaluation questionnaires and models.

Catalog of Captioned Films for the Deaf (Theatrical films and Educational Films for Adults) Prepared by the Special Materials Project of the Associations for Education of the Deaf 1981–82. Maryland: Special Materials Project, 1983. Updates issued periodically.

> A listing of films available on loan from Captioned Films for the Deaf (Indianapolis, Indiana). Includes film synopses, running time, ratings (adult, all ages, adults only, not suitable for young children), black and while or color, and date of current lease expiration.

Chandler, James G. "Voice Indexing of Tape Recordings," *Journal of Visual Impairment and Blindness.* 73(May 1979):191–192.

> A brief description of the voice indexing process, equipment needed, and its unlimited possibilities for use.

Charles, Richard. *Handicapped Programs: California Community Colleges.* 1981. ERIC Doc.No. ED 200 271.

> Examines the legal responsibility of California community colleges toward disabled persons as specified in federal and state legislation.

Cheeseman, Margaret et al. *Guidelines for Libraries to Serve Special Patrons.* Harrisburg: Pennsylvania State Library, 1977. ERIC Doc.No. ED 167 143.

> Discusses how librarians must be aware of but not overwhelmed by disabling conditions, and how disabled patrons may be accommodated through adequate physical facilities and special attention. Includes a list of information sources, as well as a list of factors which must be considered in order to adequately meet the needs of blind and deaf patrons.

"Computers and the Disabled," *Byte* 7(September 1982):136–317.

> The feature of this issue is how microcomputers can be used as aids for disabled persons. Discusses topics including: adapting equipment to give disabled persons access to standard software; speech synthesizers; and braille computer programming languages.

Coons, Maggie and Milner, Margaret. *Creating an Accessible Campus.* Washington, D.C.: Association of Physical Plant Ad-

ministrators of Universities and Colleges, 1978. ERIC Doc. No.
ED 175 080.

A guide to assist colleges in complying with Section 504 by modifying
physical structures.

Cotler, Stephen R. and DeGraff, Alfred H. *Architectural Accessibility for the Disabled of College Campuses.* New York:
State University Construction Fund, October, 1976.

A guide which provides architectural criteria toward realistic acccessibility
for disabled persons on college campuses. Includes sections on library
accessibility.

Cushman, Ruth-Carol. "The Kurzweil Reading Machine," *Wilson Library Bulletin* 54(January 1980):311–315.

Describes how the Kurzweil machine works and how it may be used.

Cylke, F. Kurt. "International Coordination of Library Services
for Blind and Physically handicapped Individuals: an Overview
of IFLA Activities," *UNESCO Journal of Information Science,
Librarianship and Archives Administration* 1(October 1979):242–
248.

A very brief overview of projects and plans of the IFLA Round Table
of Libraries for the Blind.

Cylke F. Kurt and Deschere, Allen R. "Information and Communication Devices for Blind and Physically Handicapped
Readers," *ASIS Bulletin* 5(April 1979):9–11.

A brief overview of equipment and electronic technology for use by blind
and physically disabled persons.

Cylke, F. Kurt, ed. *Library Service for the Blind and Physically
Handicapped: an International Approach: Key Papers Presented
at the IFLA Conference 1978 Strbske Pleso, CSSR.* New York:
K G Saur, 1979.

Addresses the topic of international transfer of special materials for the
blind, visually and physically disabled. Five areas are dealt with: copyright, bibliographic control; postal regulations and custom laws; format;
international and national liaison. Identifies problems and suggests solutions.

Dalton, Phyllis I. *Libraries in the United States and the International Year of Disabled Persons: Highlights of the Year—1981.* Chicago: ALA, 1982. ERIC Doc. No. ED 224 490.

A brief summary of the activities and programs developed and implemented by United States librarians during the International Year of Disabled Persons. Information given includes descriptions of the activities and the libraries in which they were held, and availability of documentation. A good source for programming ideas and resource agencies.

Deveaux, Patricia Ann. *Academic Library Service to Handicapped College and University Students.* Ph.D. Dissertation. College for Teachers of Vanderbilt University, 1982.

Eighty-four directors of academic libraries were surveyed to determine services currently being offered to physically disabled students.

Duncan, John et al. comp. "Environmental Modifications for the Visually Impaired: A Handbook," *Journal of Visual Impairment and Blindness* 71(December 1977):442–455.

Discusses kinds and sources of information that can be used in planning environmental modifications for the visually impaired. Also includes lists of sources for written information, orientation aids, and technical assistance in the United States.

Eldridge, Leslie. *Speaking out; Personal and Professional Views on Library Service for Blind and Physically Handicapped Individuals.* Washington, D.C.: Library of Congress National Library Service for the Blind and Physically Handicapped, 1982.

A compilation of interviews with librarians, students, educators, and users of library services for the blind and physically disabled concerning their thoughts and feelings about attitudes, education and experiences encountered while dealing with visual and physical disabilities.

Englebert, A. "In Sight Out: Library Service to the Deaf and Hearing Impaired," *Show-Me Librarian* 33(February 1982):20–24.

Discusses the problems of the deaf as an invisible minority who are not politically organized, and who often find it difficult to communicate with the library staff. Concludes with suggestions for librarians to use in communicating with deaf patrons.

Ensley, Robert F. ed. "Special Library Services," *Illinois Libraries* 57(September 1975):446–460.

This issue is divided into 3 sections, the first of which deals with library services to the blind and physically disabled. Includes general information applicable to all library situations.

Evenson, Richard H. and Levering, Mary Berghaus. "Equalizing Information Access by Handicapped Persons," in *Information Choices and Policies; Proceedings of the ASIS Annual Meeting, 1979*. New York: Knowledge Industry Publications, 1979, pp. 140–8.

Presents an overview of the NLS services and organizational structure, as well as new technologies in the field.

Flaningam, Donalee. *Computerized Aids for the Handicapped*. Reston, VA: National Institute of Education, 1981. ERIC Doc.No. ED 210 896.

Examines a variety of computerized aids and devices for disabled persons, as well as ways in which computers might be used in the education and employment of disabled persons. Includes a list of resources, organizations and manufacturers.

Gill, J. M. and Clark, L. L. "Resources for Creating Tactual Graphics," *Journal of Visual Impairment and Blindness* 72(January 1978):32–33.

Discusses a technique for producing tactual maps using computer assisted programs.

Goldberg, Leonard M. "Communications Technology for the Hearing Impaired," *ASIS Bulletin* 5(April 1979):12–13.

A brief overview of TTY, closed captioning, electronic mail and videodisc technology in aid to the hearing impaired.

Goss, Theresa Carter. *Model Library Services for the Hearing Handicapped*. Ed.D. Dissertation. Nova University. 1978. ERIC Doc.No. ED 167 163.

Studied 39 deaf students at the St. Petersburg (Florida) Junior College. Concludes that enhancing library services to this population would greatly increase their chances of achieving success in higher education. Special counseling, special library services and greater attention to the educational needs of hearing impaired students are recommended.

Green, Kerry. "Services for the Handicapped," *Media and Methods* 16(March 1980):39–40. ERIC Doc.No. EJ 217 595.

Suggests ways that AV personnel can meet the needs of disabled students in the areas of analyzing needs, matching needs with services, staff awareness, publicity, and recordkeeping. Includes a list of organizations that provide learning aids to disabled students.

Hagemeyer, Alice. *Deaf Awareness Handbook for Public Librarians*. Washington, D.C.: Public Library of the District of Columbia, 1975.

Although this document focuses on public library service, much of the information is applicable to all types of libraries. Includes statistics and definitions of deafness; sections on communication techniques, materials, and resources, and suggestions of special library services for the deaf.

Hagle, Alfred D. "Information access by Blind and Physically Handicapped Persons," in Wesley Simonton, ed., *Advances in Librarianship* vol. 12. New York: Academic Press, 1982, pp. 247–275.

Provides definitions and recent statistics concerning persons with visual and physical disabilities in the United States; lists and addresses of agencies that provide special library services and resources; and sections on braille electronic reading machines, paperless braille, optacon machines, braille computer terminals, voice synthesizers, speech compression, voice indexing of audio cassettees, computer-assisted lipreading for the deaf, bibliographic control of special materials, and international cooperation.

Handbook for Blind College Students, 4th ed. Baltimore: National Federation of the Blind, Students Division, 1977. Available from the Federation, 1800 Johnson St., Baltimore, MD 21230.

A handbook for disabled students. Provides suggestions and information concerning higher education and how the disabled student can facilitate his/her own optimal use of college and university services. Includes model forms and sample requests that the disabled student might provide for college and university staff to ease his/her use of the facilities and services. Also includes lists of regional libraries, braille presses, and print book enlargement agencies.

The Handicapped Student in America's Colleges: A Longitudinal Analysis. Part 3: Disabled 1978 College Freshman 3 years later. Higher Education Research Institute, Inc. Los Angeles, CA. 1982. ERIC Doc. No. Ed 226 694.

Third and final phase of a longitudinal study of college freshmen who indicated, in 1978, that they were disabled. The results of the 1981 follow-up study indicate that, given access to colleges and universities, disabled students will match the performance of non-disabled students. The study results also indicated that 1) people with different types of handicaps must be accommodated differently; 2) within disability groups, individuals will differ in their needs for physican and human accommodation; and 3) reductions in financial aid will adversely affect disabled students more than non-disabled students.

Hebert, Francoise and Noel, Wanda. *Copyright and Library Materials for the Handicapped: a Study Prepared for the International Federation of Library Associations and Institutions.* New York: K G Saur, 1982.

". . . examines the special nature of library services for the handicapped, and identifies copyright problems associated with the production and dissemination of materials in braille, audiotape and large print." (p. 7). Legislation and international copyright conventions to determine types of legislation that might resolve copyright problems are discussed. Also includes recommendations for action of IFLA.

Hopkins, Karen and Johnstone, Charles. "TDDs: What to Consider When Buying," *Interface* 4(Spring 1982):2–3.

Provides a chart of TDD devices which are currently available, along with basic information about them.

Huffman, Edythe S. *Library Services for the Deaf, Blind and Physically Disabled People in the United States, 1977–1979: An Annotated Bibliography.* Master's Thesis. University of North Carolina at Chapel Hill. 1980. ERIC Doc.No. ED 189 816.

Contains 327 items including books, articles, and AV materials, organized into sections which discuss legislation, descriptions of disabilities, technology, attitudes, education, services and resources.

Jackson, Katherine Morgan. *A Study of Accessibility of College and University Libraries to Handicapped Students Since the Re-*

habilitation Act of 1973. Ph.D. Dissertation. Texas A & M University, 1982.

Reports on information about accessibility obtained from existing printed sources concerning major construction between 1974 and 1980 at four-year colleges and universities.

Jahoda, Gerald. "Library Service to Visally Disabled College Students," *Community and Junior College Libraries* 2(Winter, 1982):21–23.

Describes the needs of visually-impaired college students and offers suggestions concerning how to meet these needs.

Jahoda, Gerald. "Suggested Goals for Public Library Service to Physically Disabled Persons," *RQ* 20(Winter 1980):149–154.

Although this article deals with public libraries, both the goals that are presented, as well as the survey instrument that is reproduced could be modified for use in an academic library setting.

Judd, P. M. "The Library and Information Needs of Visually Handicapped Students: A Survey of the Problems with Some Suggestions for Academic Library Policy," *Journal of Librarianship* 2(April 1977):96–107.

Discusses the problems of visually handicapped students; how they are being solved; and how they might be solved in British academic libraries.

Kamisar, Hylda. "Signs for the Handicapped Patron," in *Sign Systems for Libraries; Solving the Wayfinding Problem*. edited by Dorothy Pollett and Peter C. Haskell. New York: Bowker, 1979, pp. 99-103.

Provides a checklist of major design elements to be considered when developing a total guidance system.

Kepley, B. B. "Archives: Accessibility for the Disabled," *American Archivist* 46(Winter 1983):42–51.

A discussion of the special needs of disabled researchers seeking access to archival collections. Includes suggestions concerning special services which can be provided in an archival library.

Kraus, Krandall and Biscoe, Eleanor, eds. *Summary Proceedings of a Symposium on Educating Librarians and Information Scientists to Provide Information and Library Services to Blind and Physically Handicapped Individuals. July 2–4, 1981. San Francisco, California.* Washington, D.C.: Library of Congress, 1981.

Summary of conference proceedings which discussed the questions of what information needs of disabled patrons can be met by libraries; What librarian competencies will be needed to meet these needs; why should, and how can, library schools prepare librarians to meet these needs.

Lane, Elizabeth and James. "Reference Material for the Disabled," *Reference Services Review* 10(Fall 1982):73–76.

A selective bibliography of several types of reference sources which can be useful to disabled individuals.

Large Type Books in Print. New York: R. R. Bowker Company, published periodically.

Produced in large print format, this includes general reading materials and textbooks which have been produced in 14-point type or larger. Gives the same information about the books as that provided in *Books in Print.*

"LC/NLS Standards," *Interface* 5(Winter 1983):6–7.

A prepublication review of the revised *Standards of Service for the Library of Congress Network of Libraries for the Blind and Physically Handicapped (NLS Network Standards),* scheduled for adoption in late 1984.

Lende, Helga. *Books about the Blind: a Bibliographic Guide to Literature Relating to the Blind.* New York: The William Byrd Press, Inc., 1953.

One of the first attempts to list nonmedical literature related to visual impairments.

Lessee, Judith. "A Bibliography of Media Resources," *Reference Services Review* 10(Spring 1982):48–56.

An annotated review of films and other media along with comments on evaluating, locating, and utilizing media on the disabled.

"Libraries for the Blind and Physically Handicapped," in *American Library Directory*. New York: R. R. Bowker Company, published annually.

A directory of regional and subregional libraries of the Library of Congress National Library Service for the Blind and Physically Handicapped.

"Libraries Serving the Deaf and Hearing Impaired," in *American Library Directory*. New York: R. R. Bowker Company, published annually.

A selective listing of libraries in the United States which provide TTY or TDD reference service. The listing serves as a special index to the Directory.

Library Resources for the Blind and Physically Handicapped. A Directory of Division of the Blind and Physically Handicapped Network Library Libraries and Machine Lending Agencies. Washington, D.C.: Library of Congress National Library Service for the Blind and Physically Handicapped, published annually.

A directory of Network libraries and machine lending agencies in the United States.

Library Technology Reports 17(November/December 1981): entire issue.

This issue of the journal is devoted to library equipment for disabled partrons. It includes addresses, prices and detailed descriptions/evaluations of equipment for the blind, physically disabled, hearing impaired, and deaf.

"LSDS Reviews: An Occasional Publication of the Library Service to the Deaf Section," *Interface* 5(Spring 1983):12–13.

An annotated bibliography of materials dealing with deafness, sign language and aids and apppliances for the deaf. Also included are annotations of a signed film on the Jewish Sabbath; a fact sheet on hearing impaired students in post secondary education; and a periodical, *Audecibel,* for use by professionals who treat and assist the hearing impaired.

Lucas, Linda S. "Education for Library Work with Disabled and Institutionalized Persons," *Journal of Education for Librarianship* 23(Winter 1983):207–223.

Describes teaching techniques used at the University of South Carolina College of Library and Information Science to sensitize students to the problems of disabled persons. Some of the techniques described include simulations of disabilities; visits to libraries serving disabled or institutionalized persons; volunteer projects with disabled or institutionalized persons; and content analysis of fiction and nonfiction dealing with disabled persons.

McConnell, David. "Helping Students with a Disability Achieve their Academic Aims," *Studies in Higher Education* 6, no. 1(1981):35–45.

The special needs of disabled college students are examined. It is proposed that each institution of higher education have a policy statement on disabled student admission to ensure these students' welfare.

Major, Jean A. "The Visually Impaired Reader in the Academic Library," *College and Research Libraries* 39(May 1978):191–196.

The findings of a 1975 needs assessment study for the Ohio State University Library for the Blind included the need for more tape recording equipment, catalogs of materials, information about available state and local services, special reading and listening rooms, recreational and reference materials, and a register of local readers and braille transcribers.

Makas, Elaine, comp. *Attitudes and Disability: an Annotated Bibliography, 1975–1981.* Washington, D.C.: George Washington University, 1981. ERIC Doc.No. ED 218 855.

Annotates documents dealing with attitudes related to disabilities.

Marx, Pat. *The Handicapped Student on College Campuses: Advocacy, Responsibility, and Education. National Conference (3rd, Denver, Colorado, May 18–27), 1980.* ERIC Doc.No. 216 488.

Proceedings of the conference include papers on attitudes, faculty relations, delivery services, and adjustment to disabilities.

Materials from the National Arts and the Handicapped Information Service: Annotated Bibliography. Second Draft. New York: National Arts and The Handicapped Information Center, 1978. ERIC Doc.No. ED 183 158.

Describes media and materials on the subject of the arts and disabled
persons. Includes books, recordings, films, braille and large print since
1970. Does not include journals, articles, or dissertations.

MIGHT: a Guide to the University of Texas at Austin for Handicapped Students, 7th ed. University of Texas at Austin, Office
of the Dean of Students: Services for Handicapped Students,
1978.

A guide for disabled students (published by the Mobility Impaired Grappling Hurdles Together—MIGHT—student organization) at the University
of Texas at Austin, The guide not only includes physical accessibility
information, but also includes social accessibility information and delineations of teacher and counselor/student and counselee responsibilities.

Mistler, Sharon. *Planning for Implementation of Section 504 at
Colleges and Universities.* Washington, D.C.: Regional Rehabilitation Research Institute on Attitudinal, Legal and Leisure
Barriers, March, 1978. Available from the Institute, the George
Washington University, 1828 L Street, NW, Suite 704, Washington, D.C, 20036.

Provides detailed explanations and suggestions for applications in universities for each part of the Rehabilitation Act of 1973, Section 504.

Moon, I.B. "Free and Inexpensive Materials on Aids and Devices for the Physically Handicapped," *Collection Building* 4,
no. 2(1983):57–63.

An annotated bibliography of bibliographies and commercial catalogs
which list sources of information on devices and products available for
use by the physically disabled.

Moorehead, J. H. "Government Involvement In Programs for
the Handicapped," *Serials Librarian* 7(Winter 1982):7–16.

A brief discussion of Sections 503 and 504 of the 1973 Rehabilitation Act,
followed by a bibliography of bibliographies, directories and periodicals
dealing with disabilities issued by governmental agencies.

*National Organizations Concerned with Visually and Physically
Handicapped Persons.* Washington, D.C.: Library of Congress
National Library Service for the Blind and Physically Handicapped, 1980.

A directory of organizations, professional and volunteer associations, and federal agencies which offer direct and advisory services for disabled individuals.

Needham, William L. "Academic Library Service to Handicapped Students," *Journal of Academic Librarianship* 3(November 1977):273–9.

A brief version of the book listed in this bibliography under Needham and Jahoda.

Needham, William L. and Jahoda, Gerald. *Improving Library Service to Disabled Persons: A Self-Evaluation Checklist.* Colorado: Libraries Unlimited, 1983.

Major portions of the text are practical self-evaluation checklists for use by public, academic, and school librarians who wish to review and evaluate the adequacy of their libraries' resources, services, staffing, funding, facilities and public relations to and for disabled patrons. Text includes lists of organizations that provide special format materials; provide I and R services; or provide technical assistance and materials to persons with disabilities. Also includes a bibliography of professional readings; policy and job description guidelines for coordination and coordinators of library services to the physically disabled; funding strategies, standards, and legislation affecting service to this group.

Opocensky, Virginia Belle Larson. *A Comparison of Library Media Centers in Public Residential Schools for the Deaf with 'Standards for Library-Media Centers in Schools for the Deaf'. Ph.D. Dissertation. University of Nebraska. 1975.*

Obtained information on the extent to which library media centers in US public residential schools for the deaf met or failed to meet the 1967 *Standards for Library Media Centers in Schools for the Deaf.*

Parkin, Derral. *The University Library: a Study of Services Offered the Blind.* ERIC Doc.No. ED 102 972.

Surveyed 65 four-year universities in the Intermountain West concerning how many blind students they had and what services and facilities were available to them. A second survey was distributed to blind students attending Brigham Young University. An analysis of both surveys showed that full potential service to the blind is not being offered.

Peterson, Brenda and Bodenhamer, Genie. *North Texas State University Faculty Guide for Helping Handicapped Students.* Denton: North Texas State University. Office of the Dean of Students. Services to Handicapped Committee, no date of publication given.

A guide for faculty which provides useful information about disabling conditions and how to meet the special needs of disabled students.

Planning Barrier Free Libraries; a Guide for Renovation and Construction of Libraries Serving Blind and Physically Handicapped Readers. Library of Congress. National Library Service for the Blind and Physically Handicapped. Washington, D.C.: Library of Congress National Library Service for the Blind and Physically Handicapped, 1981.

A guide which suggests ways to establish renovation programs for network libraries. Space requirements, various types of equipment, and types of furniture are recommended.

Pool, Jane. *Library Services for the Blind and Physically Handicapped: a Bibliography, 1968–1979.* Washington, D.C.: Library of Congress, 1979.

This bibliography includes materials conerning library service to the blind, physically disabled, elderly, and institutionalized.

Prescott, Katherine. "New Standards for Library Service to the Blind and Physically Handicapped," *Catholic Library World* 52(November 1980):160–163.

A review and brief explanation of each area in the new standards for the NLS (see entry under American Library Association of Specialized and Cooperative Library Agencies in this bibliography) by the chair of the committee which formulated them.

Prine, Stephen and Wright, Keith C. "Standards for the Visually and Hearing Impaired," *Library Trends* 31(September 1982):93–108.

A detailed review of the development of standards for library service to the visually and hearing impaired.

Proceedings of the Institute on Library Service to the Handicapped: Instructional Material for Inclusion in the Core Curric-

ulum of Library Schools. August 27–September 1, 1978. Talla-hassee, Florida: Florida State University, 1978. ERIC Doc.No. ED 171 301.

Papers describe various aspects of library service to disabled persons. Includes sample instructional materials for library school courses, bib-liography, and annotated list of AV materials on disabilities.

Proceedings of the Johns Hopkins First National Search for Applications of Personal Computing to Aid the Handicapped. October 31, 1981. California: IEEE Computer Society, 1981.

303 pages of available computer-assisted communications technology to aid visually, physically, and hearing impaired persons. All entries include descriptions of how the technology works, how it can be used, what it cannot do, and from whom it may be obtained.

Readership Characteristics and Attitudes. Service to Blind and Physically Handicapped Users. Washington, D.C.: Market Facts Inc., 1981.

Presents findings of a 1979 survey of NLS users. The survey's objective was to develop a profile of the NLS readership that would aid the NLS in its future program planning by identifying readers' concerns and interests.

Recording for the Blind Catalog of Recorded Books, 1979/1980 with 1980/81, 1981/82, 1982/83 supplements. New York: Recording for the Blind, 1983. Catalog is published periodically.

Catalog of books recorded by Recording for the Blind and available free to blind and visually disabled persons.

Redden, Martha Ross. "Access on America's Campuses: What's the Progress and Resources," *Programs for the Handicapped* 5 (September/October, 1979) :12–20.

Provides annotated lists of associations, agencies, and resources which provide information and/or direct assistance for making institutions accessible to disabled persons.

Redmond, L. comp. *Reading, Writing, and Other Communication Aids for Visually and Physically Handicapped Persons.* Washington, D.C.: Library of Congress National Library Service for the Blind and Physically Handicapped, 1978.

This listing of products includes descriptions of the devices, prices, and addresses of the companies from which they may be obtained.

Reid, Barbara A. "Programs for Disabled Students," *New Directions for Community Colleges* 7(Fall 1979):27–34.

Describes the necessary steps in developing and implementing a comprehensive program of services to disabled students.

Resource Guide to Literature on Barrier-Free Environments with Selected Annotations. US Government Printing Office. Architectural and Transportation Barriers Compliance Board. 1980. ERIC Doc.No. ED 203 577.

Lists and annotates materials concerned with the following accessibility issues: architecture, transportation, parks and recreation, legislation, statistics, disabilities by type, attitudes, aids, and information sources.

Ross, Judi, ed. "Wisconsin Conference on Library Services," *Information: Reports and Bibliographies* 11, no. 3(1982): entire issue.

The entire issue is devoted to the topic of library services to disabled persons. Although the papers do not deal directly with academic libraries, such generally applicable issues as legislation and attitudes are covered.

Rouse, Ralph D. "Presentation on Section 504 of the Rehabilitation Act," *Journal of Education for Librarianship* 21(Winter 1981):196–207.

Provides basic information concerning the history of the Rehabilitation Act of 1973 and its impact on libraries.

Self, Phyllis C. and Bopp, Richard E. "Breaking Down Barriers," *Illinois Libraries* 63(September 1981): entire issue.

Proceedings of a 1981 workshop at the University of Illinois (entitled Breaking Down Barriers) which was directed by the Illinois Center for Rehabilitation Information. Discusses technology, library instruction for disabled persons, and special services for the deaf and hearing-impaired. Includes lists of major information centers on disabilities in the United States, and a checklist for assessing the needs of disabled users.

Selvin, Hanan C. "Some Immodest Proposals for Improving Library Services to the Blind: Reflections of a Handicapped Library

User," *Information: Reports and Bibliographies* 7, no. 2(1978):22–26.

Discusses improvements that could be made to the NLS service including: Network library 800 numbers, new technology, better public relations, and better indexing of available materials.

Senkevitch, Judith J., ed. "Information Services to Disabled Individuals," *Drexel Library Quarterly* 16(April 1980):entire issue.

Entire issue is devoted to the topic. Issues discussed include education of librarians to provide special services; architectural and program accessibility; I and R services; research and new technology; and international developments.

Senkevitch, Judith J. "Toward a National Rehabilitation Data Base," *ASIS Bulletin* 5(April 1979):14–15.

A brief discussion of the history, goals and current activities of NARIC (National Rehabilitation Information Center).

Services to the Disabled in ARL Libraries. SPEC Kit #81. Washington, D.C.: Association of Research Libraries, 1982.

Report of a survey of ARL members which shows trends in library service to disabled college students at ARL libraries. Includes planning documents, building and facilities documents, general policies and procedures statements, special services policy and publicity documents, position descriptions, brochures and a bibliography.

Smith, Lynn M. *The College Student with a Disability: a Faculty Handbook.* Washington, D.C. : US Government Printing Office, 1980. ERIC Doc. No. ED 198 766.

A guide to adjustments that may be made in the academic environment to facilitate its use by disabled students. Includes discussion of readers, recorded materials, braille, technology, accessibility, and communication aids.

Smalley, Ann Walker and Mendenhall, Kathryn. *Final Report on the State-of-the-Network: an Evaluation of NLS, the Regional Libraries, and the Multistate Centers in Relation to ALA Standards of Service for Blind and Physically Handicapped Readers to the Library of Congress National Library Service for the Blind and Physically Handicapped.* Ohio: Battelle, 1983.

The purpose of the review project was to determine the level at which the 56 NLS regional libraries, NLS and the 4 multistate centers met the *Standards of Service for the Library of Congress Network of Libraries Serving the Blind and Physically Handicapped* (see entry under American Library Association of Specialized and Cooperative Agencies in this bibliography).

Steinfeld, Edward. *Access to the Built Environment: a Review of Literature.* Washington, D.C.: US Department of Housing and Urban Development, Office of Policy Development and Research, 1979.

Discusses access as a civil right; codes and regulations pertaining to accessibility; the scope of barrier-free design; and other pertinent topics. Includes bibliographies at the end of the chapters.

Stilwell, William E. *Barriers in Higher Education for Persons with Handicaps: a Continued Challenge.* 1981. ERIC Doc. No. ED 200 155.

Survey and evaluation of the degree to which Kentucky's private and junior colleges are meeting the needs of disabled students.

Strom, Maryalls, ed. *Library Service to the Blind and Physically Handicapped.* Metuchen, NJ: Scarecrow Press, 1977.

A compilation of journal articles about the reading needs of visually and physically disabled persons.

Stovall, Carole and Sedlacek, William E. *Attitudes of Male and Female University Students toward Students with Different Physical Disabilities.* Maryland University, College Park, Counseling Center, 1981. ERIC Doc. No. ED 220 762.

Results of this study indicate that personal contacts between disabled and nondisabled students are not enough to reduce prejudice. Recommendations include the need to ensure that contacts are made under positive circumstances, preferably in a workshop format.

A Study of Handicapped Services. Charleston. S.C.: Trident Technical College, 1980. ERIC Doc No. ED 186 078.

Describes existing services to disabled students, and recommends improvements at the Trident Technical College. Includes discussion of legal and moral obligations in the areas of admissions, advisement, job placement and library services.

Thomas, James L. "College and University Library Services for the Handicapped Student in Texas: Selected Findings from a Survey," *Texas Library Journal* 56(Winter 1980):12–14.

Discusses the results of a survey of college and university libraries in Texas. The survey instrument is reproduced.

Thomas, James L. and Thomas Carol H. *Academic Library Facilities and Services for the Handicapped*. Phoenix, AZ: Oryx Press, 1981.

Lists most US libraries in post-secondary and specialized institutions and indicates which have special parking, ramps, elevators, special equipment, and staff trained to meet the special needs of disabled patrons.

Thomas, James L. and Thomas, Carol H. "A Report of the Findings from the Survey *Academic Library Facilities and Services for the Handicapped Student in the United States*," *Dikta* 7(Winter 1983):109–121.

A summary report of the survey which produced the data for *Academic Library Facilities and Services for the Handicapped*, by Thomas and Thomas (see entry in this bibliography).

Thwaits, Margaret B. *Academic Library Instruction Program for Developmentally Disabled Adults*. Colorado: Colorado State University, 1979. ERIC Doc. No. ED 205 220.

Discusses the results of a library instruction program for developmentally disabled students at Colorado State University. Includes examples of exercises used in the program.

Tickton, Sidney G. and others. *1981 Idea Handbook for Colleges and Universities: Educational Opportunities for Handicapped Students*. Washington, D.C.: Academy for Educational Development, Inc., 1981. ERIC Doc. No. ED 209 984.

A compilation of notable programs, innovative approaches and practical ideas from 166 US colleges and universities. Addresses and telephone numbers of program coordinators are included.

Vanderheiden, Gregg. "Modifying and Designing Computer Terminals to Allow Access by Handicapped Individuals," in *Clinic on Library Applications of Data Processing: Public Access to Library Automation*. Edited by J. L. Divilbiss. Urbana–

Champaign: University of Illinois, Graduate School of Library
and Information Science, 1980.

Survey and evaluation of modifications that can be made to computer
terminals to allow manipulation of the keyboard and use of displayed
output by visually, physically and cognitively disabled persons.

Velleman, Ruth A. "Library Service to the Disabled: an Annotated Bibliography of Journals and Newsletters," *Serials Librarian* 5(Winter 1980):49–60.

"This bibliography offers a basic listing of journals in the fields of medical
and vocational rehabilitation, special education, and journals written for
disabled persons themselves. Existing data bases are mentioned and the
continuing need for a central clearinghouse cited." (p. 49).

Velleman, Ruth A. *Serving Physically Disabled People: An Information Handbook for All Libraries*. New York: R. R. Bowker
Company, 1979.

General reference tool including chapters on: attitudes, public libraries,
special rehabilitation libraries, school and university libraries, and legislation. Includes detailed bibliographies.

Weber, Donald John. "Disabled Persons Support: The Serial
Literature," *Serials Review* 8(Fall 1982):25–39.

A collection of bibliographic essays which contain background information
on disabilities, annotated bibliographies, online retrieval systems and
critical reviews of significant periodical and serial resources which often
receive substandard or no indexing in common indexing sources. All
contributors are either disabled; actively involved the area of "Rehabilitation Librarianship"; or working as professionals in the rehabilitation
field.

Weber, Donald John. "Periodicals Supporting Library Service
for the Blind and Physically Handicapped," *Serials Review*
7(April/June 1981):45–47.

An annotated list of primary print periodicals published in support of
library service for the physically disabled.

Weinberg, Belle. "The Kurzweil Machine: Half a Miracle,"
American Libraries 11(November 1980):603–604, 627.

A research project at the New York Public Library suggested that the Kurzweil machine will fail to reach its potential audience of blind readers unless abundant library staff support is provided.

Wexler, Henrietta. "Books that Talk," *American Education* 17(January-February 1981):15–17.

A brief overview of the history and current services of the Library of Congress National Library Service for the Blind and Physically Handicapped, as well as the Recording for the Blind.

Whalen, Lucille and Miller, Joan A. "Library Services for the Adult Handicapped: an Institute for Training in Librarianship," *Information: Reports and Bibliographies* 7, no. 2(1978):entire issue.

Proceedings from an institute held at the School of Library and Information Science, State University of New York At Albany, October 9–14, 1977. Includes articles concerning history of library service to the disabled; the psychology of disabilities; expectations of library service; attitudes toward the disabled; legislation; and resources and services.

Wilkinson, Rosalyn, ed. *Everything You Wanted to Know about Handicapped Students (and Were Not Afraid to Ask)* New York: State University of New York, Buffalo, 1981. ERIC Doc. No. 207 382.

A guide for faculty which provides information concerning how to make accomodations for disabled students in academic courses and programs.

Wilson, Betty-Ruth. *Accessibility on the Campus; Architectural Barriers and the Disabled Student, 1970–1980, An Annotated Bibliography*. Monticello, IL: Vance Bibliographies, 1982.

Annotated bibliography of materials about accessibility for disabled students on college campuses.

Wright, Keith C. *Library and Infromation Services for Handicapped Individuals*. Colorado: Libraries Unlimited, 1979.

Provides general information conerning library service to blind; physically disabled; mentally handicapped; and aged patrons. Also includes sections on legislation and definitions of specific disabling conditions.

Wright, Keith C. and Davie, Judith F. *Library and Information Services for Handicapped Individuals*. Second Edition. Colorado: Libraries Unlimited, 1983.

This second edition of Keith Wright's invaluable reference tool defines the major handicapped groups; review legal implications; presents ideas for library programs and services; and identifies sources of further information. This edition adds chapters on the speech impaired, as well as how librarians may examine their own attitudes and confront prejudice toward disabled persons.

Wright, Keith C. "Library Education and Handicapped Individuals," *Journal of Education for Librarianship* 21(Winter 1981):183–195.

Discusses the impact of Section 504 of the Rehabilitation Act of 1973 in the area of library education. Focuses on needed modifications in curricula, media formats, access to programs and services, ans stereotyped attitudes toward disabled persons by faculty, students and their professional peers.

BIOGRAPHICAL SKETCHES OF THE CONTRIBUTORS

Scott Bruntjen, Executive Director of the Pittsburgh Regional Library Center, is the author of *Data Conversion, Knowledge Industries, 1983* and *Douglas C. McMurtrie: Bibliographer and Historian of Printing* (Scarecrow Press, 1979). Formerly, he was a member of the library faculty of Shippensburg University of Pennsylvania.

Rolf M. Fuhlrott, Bibliotheksdirecktor at Karlsruhe University Library, has his doctorate in architecture from that university. Active in the International Federation of Library Associations, he is a member of the Section on Library Buildings and Equipment. Similarly, he recently was chairman of the Committee on Library Building of the German Library Institute. He is the author of several articles and books on library building problems and is founding editor of "ABI-Technik," the German library journal which covers automation, building and technology in the field of Archives, Libraries and Information Science.

Sylvia D. Hall, Development Officer of the Pittsburgh Regional Library Center, is a doctoral candidate at the University of Pittsburgh School of Library and Information Science. She was the former Director of Library Development for the State Library of Pennsylvania. Her primary interests are system development and cooperative processing of library materials.

Helen Carol Jones, Assistant Professor and Reference Librarian in the Pullen Library of Georgia State University, has interests in bibliographic instruction and reference service. In 1984 she participated in a Reference Management Workshop where she assisted in the presentation of a session on "Stress at the Reference Desk."

Michael E. D. Koenig, is Associate Professor, School of Library Service, Columbia University. A prolific author, he writes about information systems, long range planning and research productivity.

Larry N. Osborne, Assistant Professor in the Graduate School of Library Studies at the University of Hawaii, has an interest in human aspects of automation. Formerly head cataloger at Carlow College, Pittsburgh, Pa., he now teaches cataloging and classification, and systems analysis.

Ruth J. Person, Associate Dean of the School of Library and Information Science, is author of The Management Process: A Selection of Readings, American Library Association, 1983. She received a Council on Library Resources grant in 1984, and was a program speaker at the American Library Association's national conference, 1984. She has a special interest in women's roles in management. Recently, she was appointed a Commissioner of the Anne Arundel County, Md., Commission for Women.

Roscoe Rouse, Jr., Dean of Library Services, Oklahoma State University, is a frequent author on library topics. He is active in the American Library Association where he is a member of the Library Administration and Management Association Building and Equipment Section.

Ralph E. Russell, University Librarian at Georgia State University, earned his doctoral degree at Florida State University.

He has written and spoken on a variety of library topics, particularly collection development and staff development. His service to the profession includes membership on the Board of Directors of the Southeastern Library Network and chairmanship of that board 1979–81, and membership on several committees of the Association of College and Research Libraries and the Library Administration and Management Association. He serves as a consultant occasionally.

Rashelle Schlessinger Karp, Assistant Professor in the College of Library Science, Clarion University of Pennsylvania, was formerly State Librarian for the Blind in the Rhode Island Department of State Library Services. Currently a doctoral candidate at Florida State University's School of Library and Information Studies, her major interests are library automation and information science, and library service to the blind and other physically disabled. She is a contributor to professional library literature.

Barbara J. Smith, Assistant Dean of Libraries, Pennsylvania State University is chair of the Association of College and Research Libraries' Standards and Accreditation Committee 1984–1986. Also head of the Commonwealth Campus Division of the libraries, she has written on the subject of bibliographic instruction.

Deidre C. Stam, Assistant Professor in Columbia University's School of Library Service, conducts research in library management and scholarly communication. A former reference librarian at the State University of New York Purchase Campus, she has served as executive secretary of the Bibliographical Society of America.

AUTHOR INDEX

223

SUBJECT INDEX

229

FOUNDATIONS IN LIBRARY AND INFORMATION SCIENCE

A Series of Monographs Texts and Treatises

Edited by **Robert D. Stueart,** *Dean Graduate School of Library and Information Science, Simmons College, Boston*

GOVERNMENT INFORMATION QUARTERLY

An International Journal of Resources, Services, Policies, and Practices

Peter Hernon, *Editor*
University of Arizona

Charles R. McClure, *Associate Editor*
University of Oklahoma

Announces a Special Symposium Issue on

THE DECENNIAL CENSUS, U.S. BUREAU OF THE CENSUS

Volume 2, Number 4, November 1985

This special issue is the most comprehensive and prevalent commentary of the Decennial Census Program. How Census Bureau planners gain a sense of public opinion on census issues and thereby develop a concept of what the census should be is the theme of the articles. This is a process that has not been documented in as unified a manner as done in this issue.

The seven articles, submitted by top personnal within the bureau, report:

- the increasing reliance the nation places on census data described within the framework of five major uses
- the birth of the census and its development is recounted in an historical perspective
- an inside look at census planning
- Census Bureau planning activities for the redistricting data program and the role of census data in the apportionment and districting process
- how the concept of confidentiality has developed since the first census and what it means today
- census data dissemination
- the international diversity of census taking and the role our country plays in the international round of censuses.

The authors include the Census Bureau's current Director, Dr. John Keane, and the person in charge of the 1990 census, Peter A. Bounpane.

Copies of the special November issue or subscriptions to Government Information Quarterly may be obtained by writing to JAI PRESS, Inc., Subscription Department, 36 Sherwood Place, P.O. Box 1678, Greenwich, Connecticut 06836-1678. Subscription rates (postage included): Members of GODORT, ALA, $25.00; Institutions, $45.00; Individuals, $30.00. All subscriptions must be prepaid and are for the 1985 calendar year only.

 **JAI PRESS INC.**

36 Sherwood Place, P.O. Box 1678, Greenwich, Connecticut 06836-1678